MY STORY
TO HIS GLORY

MY STORY TO HIS GLORY

By Lester Sumrall

Thomas Nelson Publishers
Nashville

Published in Nashville, Tennessee, by Thomas Nelson Inc. and distributed in Canada by Lawson Falle, Ltd., Cambridge, Ontario.

Printed in the United States of America.

All Scripture quotations are from the King James Version of the Bible.

Library of Congress Cataloging in Publication Data

Sumrall, Lester Frank, 1913-
  My story to his glory.

  1. Sumrall, Lester Frank, 1913-   . 2. Evangelists—United States—Biography. I. Title.
BV3785.S78A35   1983   269.2'0924 [B]   83-8063
ISBN 0-8407-5837-5

Contents

**In gratitude to God
and
with deepest appreciation to
the members and families of
Christian Center Church**

Anything that is done for God should be centered in the church of Jesus Christ. Jesus said the gates of hell will not prevail against *His church*. To be supported and backed up by a strong church has been necessary for all our ministry outreach. God has given us a great congregation that knows how to pray and exercise faith. The Christian Center Church family, backing me in everything I undertake, gives me a tremendous sense of strength and oneness. Certainly one of the greatest blessings of my life is the privilege God has given me to be the shepherd of these beautiful people. It is a great joy to know that the total outreach of this ministry flows through a branch of the church of the Lord Jesus Christ. I want to take this means to acknowledge their faithful support and the demonstration of their Christ-like love in so many ways. My gratitude to God and to them is great.

1

Miracles Belong to God

"Are you Lester Sumrall?"

From looking at the pearls in the showcase, I looked up at the tall man asking the question and replied yes. I'm often stopped and asked that question, but what made this so unusual was that I was in the world's largest department store in downtown Tokyo, Japan.

Manfred Sobottka towered over me. He was a large man with a soft voice. "I watch you every week on television here in Tokyo. You are almost my only source of spiritual blessing."

I straightened up to look at this well-groomed businessman. "I am president of a cosmetic firm here in the city," he said, "but I am of German background." We shook hands, and he explained that he had lived in Tokyo for a number of years, that he truly loved God, and that my teachings were a much-welcomed source of blessing and help to him.

As we parted company that day, I shook my head in wonder. I will never cease being amazed at the miracle of television. Here I stood in a city of over twelve million on the main floor of this incredibly large department store, and someone tapped me on the shoulder having recognized me. What brought about this recognition? Television.

I have preached in Japan since 1936, but now I reach more people through the miracle of television than I ever reached in the many small churches I visited on my periodic journeys.

In the Philippines I had the privilege of starting a church and participating in a spiritual revival that the Lord mightily blessed. But even though thousands were being reached, it was small compared to the multiplied thousands who are now seeing the television programs.

For years the soles of my shoes slapped the streets in the world's great cities and tiny villages as I responded to God's call upon my life, which came when I was still a very young man. I've preached the gospel in over a hundred countries and have ministered in more than a thousand of the world's cities.

The first method of reaching the masses through the media was, of course, the printed word. Until about four hundred years ago, every book in the world was handwritten; but that changed with the miracle of the printing press. And the first thing printed was the Bible. At that time only 15 percent of the world's population was literate. Books were very expensive and could only be found in libraries or the collections of very rich people. In time this changed, and books became the possession of the common people as well. But many poor people never saw a book of any kind, let alone owned one.

Now literacy is common. Printed material floods the

world. I'm grateful that God has prompted me to write more than forty books and booklets, each promoting the gospel message. Hundreds of thousands of them have been sold or given away; many have been translated into foreign languages and distributed worldwide. At LeSea, our ministry headquarters in South Bend, Indiana, we keep three presses going in our print shop. We print our monthly magazine, *World Harvest*, booklets, teaching syllabuses, pamphlets, tracts, and newsletters.

When I was a small boy, radio was an innovation. Everybody was excited about this new marvel. Now it has become commonplace; everyone takes the radio for granted. But it is a great tool for spreading the gospel, and we have been in full-time gospel radio ministry since January 1968.

On Easter Sunday 1969, we dedicated our South Bend facilities, a miraculous provision of God—the Christian Center Church and LeSea (Lester Sumrall Evangelistic Association). Then we broadened our scope by incorporating the World Harvest Advanced School of Evangelism in 1971 to train pastors, missionaries, and evangelists to minister worldwide. In 1976 the School of Evangelism became World Harvest Bible College, a four-year resident training school, to better meet the needs of students.

But deep in my heart was this burning desire to reach out to the millions. How could one church do this?

As a young man just starting out, after eighteen months of preaching, God miraculously changed the course of my ministry—and my life. God gave me a vision of the world traveling on the Road of Life, the end of which was eternal destruction in a burning hell.

Perhaps you've never read anything about me, but you've picked up this book out of curiosity. You may be thinking, "That's pretty dramatic, Mr. Sumrall. Are you sure you *really* had that kind of vision?"

I can assure you that while I was sitting to the side of the pulpit in a little frame church building in the Tennessee countryside on December 18, 1931, I experienced this vision of an uncountable multitude of humankind traveling down a highway that ended abruptly at a precipice towering above a bottomless inferno. When this unending procession of people from every nation on the face of the earth came to the end of that highway, I could see them falling off into eternity.

I wasn't aware of the people in that little church, the songs they were singing, or anything that was going on around me. I was only conscious of the screams of damned souls sinking into hell. In that vision, as God drew me nearer so I could see men and women plunging into that awful chasm, I saw their faces distorted with terror, their hands flailing wildly, clawing at the air and each other.

As I looked on in stunned silence, God spoke to me out of that frightening chaos: "You are responsible for these who are lost."

I backed away, crying out, "No, not me, Lord. I don't know these people. I've never been to Japan, the Philippines, China, or India. How can I be held responsible?"

The voice of the Lord was tender, yet firm. "When I say unto the wicked, Thou shalt surely die; and thou givest him not warning, nor speakest to warn the wicked from his wicked way, to save his life; the same wicked man shall die in his iniquity; but his blood will I require at thine hand."

Not until later did I discover that this was a passage in the

Bible (from Ezek. 3:18). God left no doubt in my mind, showing me that I was responsible for turning a million souls from *that* road to the Road of Life that leads to the cross of Jesus Christ and to Christ Himself, who is the way to eternal life.

That can make a preacher out of you in a hurry! It did me! But God equipped me for this call to be a world missionary by inciting in me a hunger for His Word, by empowering me with the Holy Spirit, by blessing me with the prayers of some of His saints—Howard Carter, Donald Gee, Smith Wigglesworth, and Dr. Lillian Yeomans, to name just a few—and by opening doors of service. Then He gave me a fearless faith to believe that what He was leading me to do, He would implement *and* sustain.

Because of the vision and the call of God on my life, I was able to pioneer and establish churches in England, Alaska, Hong Kong, the Philippines, Israel, Brazil, Australia, and the United States. These churches send out missionaries and evangelists to keep spreading the Good News that Jesus Christ is Lord.

It was, therefore, somewhat difficult for me to understand at first why God would take me from the mission field to begin a work in South Bend, Indiana. But then I began to understand as I became very still and sensitive to the leading of the Lord. God seemed to be saying to me, "America is in worse shape than even the people in the Philippines." (We were ministering in the church in Manila at the time.)

I read the newspaper and magazine accounts of the violence rampant at political rallies, conventions, and on university campuses across the land. Surely the news in the mid-1960s did not make for pleasant reading or listening. The drug culture was rapidly becoming a fact of life, and it seemed that every city and town was affected. The sexual revolution looked like a scourge bent on destroying America. Pornography was filling the newsstands; material greed had taken hold; unrestrained madness appeared to be taking over the minds and hearts of my fellow countrymen. I remember saying to my wife, "The United States is in worse condition than the Philippines or many of the places where we've ministered." And so it was that we returned to South Bend with a sense of divine destiny.

My wife, Louise, and I talked about this new direction our ministry was taking. We knew that we would continue to travel around the world in pursuit of souls, but for the rest of our lives our base of operations would be America.

I, like so many others, had been keeping my eye on television for a number of years. When television first came on the scene in 1946, there were only six stations telecasting to a few thousand sets. It has since grown fantastically. In the mid-1960s, 750 TV stations were telecasting to about 62 million sets in the United States. By then it had literally invaded the home. The major networks were already broadcasting most programs in color. Television had certainly come a long way. At the same time cable TV came into its own, delivering programs to hard-to-reach places, such as deep valleys. Cable TV has been a real boon to religious telecasting.

God led us to further the spread of the gospel through television in 1972—first in Indianapolis, then in 1976 in Miami, Florida, and in 1978 in South Bend. When we responded to the desperate cry for Christian TV programming, there were only five or six such stations in the world. Today there are still only about a dozen, and we still have two of them.

How could God take me, coming from a mission field with a small salary and no denominational backing or major church support, and enable me to develop this television ministry? Well, that's just it—it isn't just me, although God has allowed me to be a sort of catalyst to help bring it all about. But I knew that one man and a small church group could never reach a million souls quickly. The mass media were needed to help get the job done. And there must be thousands of financial *and* prayer partners helping to utilize this space-age technology.

And that's what has happened. People responded to this new work that God laid upon my heart and theirs. Today we are on two satellites, and we have our own cable stations. Our ministry is able to reach the whole North American continent via these systems. And that's just at the time of this writing. We are trusting God for an ever widening outreach as God's people link hearts and hands to win a million to Christ.

We're not limiting God, of course. A million souls is a lot of people. A million souls is not a number, it is flesh-and-blood human beings headed for a Christless eternity whom we want to reach—before it is too late for them and they become part of that vast multitude I long ago saw plunging into hell.

2

Fearless Faith

As a seventeen-year-old boy, I lay on my deathbed in our home in Panama City, Florida, slowly succumbing to the ravages of tuberculosis. The doctor's visits had been frequent but futile. One fateful afternoon, I started to choke and turn blue in the face. I'd been spitting blood every day for weeks, but now I was hemorrhaging. "The boy is as good as dead now," I heard the doctor tell my mother. "Call your husband. This boy is dying."

It's an awful feeling to know you are dying and you aren't ready to die. I wanted to live. I wanted to be a businessman. I had goals of making a lot of money and being very successful. Death was the furthest thing from my mind.

For months mother had been bringing in her "Prayer Meeting Group" to pray over me. They were persistent, standing around the bed, pleading with the Lord to spare my life. I begged my mother to call off her prayer partners. "Don't bring that bunch of old women back here anymore," I kept saying. But the next week they'd be back. Under the covers I cussed at them.

But this day was different. I was hovering between life and death, yet I knew what was going on. My parents were crying, even my six-foot-three Irish father. Then it happened. At that moment God gave me a vision. (It was the first of two visions I've had in my life; the other vision was related in the previous chapter.) On one side of my bed I saw a coffin—just my size, open and tilted, very pretty inside, but empty, waiting for me to die. There was no mistaking it, this coffin was meant for me. I turned my head the other way. I didn't want to look at that casket. But on the other side of my bed I saw a Bible. It reached from the floor to the ceiling. It was the biggest Bible in the world. Then I heard God say, "That's My Word. You have a choice. Lester, which of these will you choose *tonight?*"

It wasn't an audible voice, yet it was as distinct and as firm a voice as any I'd ever heard. But I didn't want to be a preacher. Many times I'd heard my mother sob, "Lord, save Lester and make him a preacher." I hated evangelists and called them names. I had determined I wasn't going to be one of them.

There was a struggle. While my family stood around crying, wringing their hands and waiting for me to die, I was fighting it out with God. I wanted to live, so I pleaded with God. "Lord, I'm afraid to die. I'm not ready to die. God, if the only way in the world for me to live is to preach—I'll preach." I asked God to give me a long life of preaching and promised Him that I'd never stop preaching as long as there was a breath in me.

It was settled. Just that quickly the vision vanished. I

recall drifting into a deep sleep. I'd made a commitment to God, and I'd surrendered my heart to Jesus Christ. The covenant was sealed. My destiny had been determined.

Morning was like resurrection. No blood stained my pillow. No pain racked my chest. No fever chilled my skin and burned my brain. When I opened my eyes, the first person I saw was my blurry-eyed mother.

I asked for food and told her about the vision and my promise to God. Mother cried out, "Oh, God, can it be? Can it be?" Three days later I was walking all over the house, and three weeks later I walked out of the house with all my earthly belongings.

God has always spoken to me from His Word. I don't just close my eyes, open the Bible, and say, "What do You have for me, Lord?" His Word to me is always specific. That day I knew I was to turn to Isaiah 41:10–11. When I told my father I was going to preach, he reacted with rage. He snorted, raved, and threatened. Obviously, my father wasn't a Christian. But God had started something in me, and He has kept it up through all these years. I knew I had to be obedient to His Word. I spread my Bible open before me on the floor and there I read:

> Fear thou not; for I am with thee: be not dismayed; for I am thy God: I will strengthen thee; yea, I will help thee; yea, I will uphold thee with the right hand of my righteousness. Behold, all they that were incensed against thee shall be ashamed and confounded: they shall be as nothing; and they that strive with thee shall perish.

Moments before fear had gripped me with paralyzing force. Then suddenly, it was as if I had felt a hand go down through my mouth and into that region that was the source of my fear. It was as if a turnip had been pulled up out of a patch with little tendrils hanging down. As I read "Fear thou *not* . . . ," the fear was gone.

The Bible says, "God hath not given us the spirit of fear; but of power, and of love, and of a sound mind" (2 Tim. 1:7). Fear is a spirit. I felt its presence leave. For years I've been preaching and telling people they don't have to be under bondage to this spirit of fear. I can preach that because I've experienced what it is to be released from fear.

When fear is relinquished, in its place can come fearless faith. Up until that time my one great fear was my father. Physically, I'm not a big man; but my father was. He had muscles that stood up like an arch. He prided himself in the way he could flex those muscles. It terrified me. More than once I'd felt the brute power of his physical strength.

My father had shouted at me that if I left home I'd starve to death. As I read over those verses in Isaiah, I began to laugh. It was a kind of holy hilarity. It was exciting. I reread those promises in Isaiah 41:10–11. And those two verses have been a cornerstone, an anchorage in my life from that moment until now. In every crisis in my life, they have risen up to help and encourage me. "Fear thou not . . . I *am* with thee."

After packing my little, old, fiberboard suitcase, I came marching down the steps and was met by my mother. She'd heard me sobbing upstairs, and then she'd sensed that God was doing something. "Where are you going, Lester?" she asked.

"I'm leaving to preach."

She started to cry, and I said, "Mother, you cried for years because I wasn't saved; you cried when I got saved.

You prayed for years that I'd be a preacher; now I'm going to do it and you're crying again."

"Oh, Lester," she said through her sobs, "these are tears of joy. I know God will take care of you."

I never returned to that little home. I cut my roots and walked away with only sixty-five cents in my pocket. I was walking into the Great Depression of the thirties as far as the world was concerned, but I didn't realize it. I left home believing that God was God and that everything would be all right. It was my first real act of faith.

I had a lot to learn in those early days of brush-arbor preaching in the back country of Florida and Tennessee. I began to learn that when you feed your faith, you starve your doubts. I couldn't have put it into words at that point, but later I would look back and be able to articulate what I'd gone through earlier. I pray that my story of God's faithfulness will help to ignite your faith. But know this for a fact—all lack of faith is due to not feeding on God's Word. How can *you* enter into the abundant life of faith? It will come as you feed on the living Christ. "Faith cometh by hearing, and hearing by the word of God" (Rom. 10:17).

3

The World Didn't Seem to Need Me

When I was born, our house was already full of children. There were Houston, Anna, Kerney, Ernest, Louise—and now there was Lester. I wasn't really needed. As I grew up, I often felt this.

When I started out to preach, there were literally hundreds of young men and women on the evangelistic circuit and out in the mission fields of the world. They all seemed much better suited for the ministry than I. This world didn't seem to need me either.

When I became a missionary, it seemed that the field was overrun with workers. I knew my lack of training and my little experience hardly qualified me for the mission field. Was I really needed?

The first eighteen months away from home as a young preacher-boy were my introduction into the school of evangelism. Sometimes I go over to our World Harvest Bible College and observe those young men and women deep in study, and I am reminded of my own preparation. It was far different from this. Then I am overwhelmed with gratitude to the Lord and His faithful people who have helped make this arm of our ministry possible.

When I wrote my first book and offered it to Marshall, Morgan, and Scott in London, England, my friends told me there were already enough authors and books. I wasn't needed.

It was only Jesus who made me feel wanted *and* needed. He gave assurance that I had a place among men. This place has often been challenged. There are those who would try to wrench away a man's faith and his call.

A fishing buddy joined me as we left Panama City those long years ago. We headed north in his old Overland car. Our faith and spirits were high as we stopped under a persimmon tree after traveling some distance and ate our fill. I didn't look like a preacher in my ninety-two pounds of city-boy finery, but I did manage to convince farmers along the way to open up their old country schoolhouses and let us hold revival services. Most of the time we found these schoolhouses had no electricity, so we had to borrow lanterns.

A meeting of any kind in the country in those days was a social event. The farmers and their wives welcomed opportunities to come together and talk about their crops and the things farmers' wives talk about. Their sons and daughters came to look each other over. So it was a sort of social thing, but we did manage to get a congregation together. I wouldn't want you to think my preaching was so dramatic that *it* was causing the people to turn out!

We held many open-air revivals under arbors—shelters made from branches of trees. I still marvel that the Lord could have used me at all. I stood before those farmers and their families in my white shirt, white trousers, white socks, and white shoes; and I didn't have a lot of love in my heart for those people. I worked hard and was faithful to my calling, but still I had a bad attitude. I wasn't as clean on the inside as I looked on the outside.

At times I was brash, abrupt, and negative. Often the response was laughter. This irritated me. I tried to tell them the story of Lester Sumrall, living, dying, and living again. They hee-hawed. I was pretty frustrated. But I had to fulfill my obligation to God. I'd made a promise. God had spared my life. And to tell the truth, I didn't want to risk almost dying again. The next time I spoke I decided to try a new approach. "Let me tell you why I'm here. I was born in New Orleans into a half-Christian family. My mother is a Christian, but my father is not."

"Haw, haw, haw!" The laughing started again. The farmers would chew and then spit their tobacco juice and laugh at me. I was miserable but determined to tell my story.

I told them about my frequent brushes with death—the time a few years after birth when I contracted the dread disease pellagra. Mother's prayer group prayed for me, and God answered with a miracle. God's cure left no defects from the ravaging disease. Then there was the time, at the age of five or six, when my oldest brother, Houston, and I were playing on a railroad switching track near our home. Without warning this brother, who was more than twice my size, lunged into me; and together we rolled off the track just inches ahead of the sharp steel wheels of an engineless freight car bearing down upon us.

But that wasn't all. I spoke of the time a few years later when I narrowly escaped death by drowning. The normally calm waters of Tallahala Creek were swollen by winter rains; but when I was challenged to swim across, I took the dare. My two stronger companions made it across, but I was no match for that swollen stream. One of the kids dived in and felt along the sandy creek bottom and found me. With a desperate struggle he dragged me onto the bank. The poor kid didn't know anything about artificial respiration, but he just turned me over and kept punching me until mud and water gushed out and I gasped for air.

Things were a bit more calm after that until I reached my teen years. I once flirted with death then, too, running through the streets of Mobile, Alabama, at Mardi Gras time. A little girl in a weird costume came up and hit me, and I spun around and walloped her. The guy with her pulled out a long razor and slashed out at me, cutting through my thick sweater and shirt. (Obviously, I lived to tell about it!)

Then I moved into the story of my more recent brush with death, when I lay dying from tuberculosis. I told how God raised me up and gave me a vision, and how I promised him I'd be a preacher.

I shared with those country folk that my mother, from my earliest remembrance, knew God and was a woman of remarkable faith. But my father wasn't the least bit religious and, in fact, hated church. Mother had God and Papa had muscle, about two-hundred pounds of it. He smoked, drank, chewed tobacco, and committed adultery. My brothers, sisters, and I were fearful of this godless man. We tried to keep on his good side because he was so strong. When you got spanked by Papa, you saw stars and stripes. We kept things right with him even if we had to tell a lie now and then. When his fists hit the table, the dishes flew. He cussed me for everything you could cuss a poor kid for. He made threats and would slam the back door as he left home, yelling at the top of his lungs. His whippings and tongue lashings really hurt. When Papa was especially angry, instead of calling me "Lester," he would boom out with "Boy!" That was warning enough for me.

Early in life, I discerned the dissension in my family. "Mother is religious," I decided. "If I want to go that way, I have to be good. But Papa is a sinner. If I want to go that way, I can do anything I want to do!" I decided to go Papa's way, but I had not taken into account Mother and her friends from the ladies' prayer group.

Mother kept all her children clean, well-dressed, well-fed, in church, and in line. She never sought for Papa's assistance in discipline. Since I was the meanest kid in the family, she whipped me more than all the others put together. At least that's the way it seemed to me. Once she even threatened to send me to a reform school. To my knowledge she never communicated this to Papa. He just might have done it. I think that's what worried her and stopped her from suggesting it!

When I was about six years old, there was fear in our house. We felt that our mother was going to die. An open, draining cancer on her left breast kept her in constant pain. In those days the doctors knew only one thing to do about cancer. They cut it out with a knife. "I don't want to touch it," the family doctor told her and Papa. "We never get the roots, and it will just come back worse than ever. We'll operate only if you insist." Neither Mother nor Papa insisted.

One night Mother walked the floor in pain and in

exhaustion fell across the bed. Then, not knowing whether it was a dream or a vision, she saw Jesus enter her room and put His finger on her chest. When she woke up, she told my father of her dream and that the pain was gone. A few days later my father asked her about the sore and she checked the dressing, which was usually damp with fluid and blood. Suddenly she shrieked with amazement and joy. In the gauze lay something that looked like a baby octopus, a black core with tentacles. The cancer lay there in her hand. In the mirror she saw new flesh and skin. She was healed! My mother lived another forty-five years and died at the age of eighty-seven.

That wasn't the only miracle of healing that I saw take place as a child. We were living in Laurel, Mississippi, when a policeman friend brought my Grandpa Chandler to us one day in the back seat of his car. Grandpa had been felled in the street by a massive stroke. My Uncle Charlie wanted to take him to the hospital, but Mother wanted to pray. Uncle Charlie did get him to the hospital, but not out of the car. The family doctor came out and said, "The hospital is overcrowded. Every bed is taken." And he climbed into the car to look Grandpa over. He climbed back out, shook his head, and said, "Take him home. There's nothing I can do for him here. He won't live more than a few days." Mother had already moved into action and had called her ladies' prayer group. Grandpa was so limp that the men had to tie him into a straight chair in order to carry him into the house.

The ladies arrived and began praying in earnest. When these ladies prayed, the neighborhood knew about it. "What's that racket?" one neighbor asked my sister.

"Grandpa had a stroke, and Mother's ladies' prayer

group is praying. Jesus is going to heal him," my sister responded.

"Nonsense," the neighbor said.

"No," my sister insisted. "Grandpa is going to be healed."

The neighbor walked back into his house, shaking his head and holding his hands to his ears. Meanwhile, Grandpa fell asleep. When he awoke, he moved his arms. Then he moved his legs. He called out to my mother, "Betty, where are my clothes?" Before any of us knew what was happening, he was out of bed, dressing himself. The neighbor was out in his yard. When he saw my grandfather he began to weep. As a result of that, this neighbor came to Christ. Seeing a miracle like that doesn't always result in someone's believing in Christ, but it should put the fear and love of God in one's heart. In spite of the miracles, however, my father still resisted the Lord.

And so did those country folk. As I related these things, most of them seemed unaffected by my story. Often the evening ended on a sorry note. One night I was so dejected that I didn't even try to take an offering, and I didn't ask anyone if they wanted to be saved either. The next morning the host-farmer said, "Young man, if you don't work, you don't eat. If you plan to stay here any longer, you can feed the hogs!"

Feed the hogs? Glancing down at my clean hands and clothes, my heart sank. "Feed the hogs?" I said it aloud.

"Yes, don't it say in the Bible that if you don't work, you don't eat?"

"But I *am* working. Preaching is working."

"No, it ain't!" he said, and with that he shoved two big pails of slop into my hands. "Go feed my pigs."

What an education! As I carried those heavy buckets, the foul-smelling slop sloshed over onto my clothes and into my shoes. But more than my clothes and shoes were affected. Oh, how my pride was injured. I was upset with God and angry at the world, and I didn't know how to handle it. I lay down in the middle of the corn field, not caring if my clothes were getting dirty, and cried out, "Oh, Lord, maybe I should go home and die! Anything, Lord—but not this!"

After that I was really able to identify with the story of the Prodigal Son. As I lay there, humiliated and weeping, I sensed that God was trying to teach me something. "If you will be faithful to Me, Lester, in the little things, I will give you bigger things. If you won't quit, I'll let you touch many people by My power; and you will yet bless multitudes."

I lay there quietly crying while the realization began to sweep over me that God hadn't deserted me. He wasn't punishing me. He was only training me to be useful to Him.

After a while I got up, picked up the empty buckets, and carried them back to the barn. I drew water from the well, washed my foul-smelling clothes, took a crude sort of bath, and began to study the Bible in earnest. I had to learn how to preach to these people. I began to realize that I really was needed after all.

4

Chosen, Anointed, and Sent

I stayed with those country folk a while longer, moving north to Tennessee and Arkansas. I saw them finally come around, responding to the moving of the Holy Spirit as the country-boy preacher preached his heart out. The vision of an uncountable multitude on the road to hell changed me. I asked God to forgive me for my former treatment of people, and I experienced the wonderful feeling of knowing my spirit and soul had truly been cleansed. I was set free. Like the Prodigal Son who came to his senses and experienced his father's forgiveness and love, I knew I was the recipient of our heavenly Father's outpoured forgiveness and love. Romans 8:1 became real in my life: "There is therefore now no condemnation to them which are in Christ Jesus, who walk not after the flesh, but after the Spirit."

For some months I had been seeking for the baptism in the Holy Ghost. I was well-acquainted with the doctrine through my mother's church and hearing her pray in an unknown tongue. But this blessing had not fallen on me.

Desperately I sought for it; yet in my heart I rebelled because I sensed that gifts from God are just that—you don't have to go around pumping yourself up into an emotional frenzy. And you don't *earn* the Holy Ghost. Then one evening after preaching, as I lay on my bed staring up at the ceiling, the glory of the Lord came into that room as I had never felt it before; and God filled me by His grace.

I remained faithful to my calling as a preacher, but I was a changed man. The combination of experiences related here, and others, infused me with a compassion and an urgency for souls that would never fade. My preaching possessed a new authority, yet there was a tenderness that had been missing before.

The young man who had accompanied me on my initial sojourn out into the world had fallen in love with a young woman along the way, gotten married, and was no longer my traveling companion. My sister Leona came and joined me in evangelistic meetings in one community after another.

Unusual and glorious things happened during those meetings. God was moving in miraculous ways. But even in the midst of revival, there were those who turned their backs on God and resisted the tug of the Holy Spirit. And on two occasions, people who willfully rejected God came to sudden, tragic ends that I believe were God's judgment on their rebellion against Him.

In one place a dairyman, who attended the services almost every night but would not yield his life to the Lord, was hit by a truck and killed instantly. When I had pleaded with him to come to God, his answer had always been the same: "No, I have just a few more things to straighten out first. I need a little more time." And then his time ran out.

In another place an insolent young man came to an abrupt ending. He had stood outside the church with other young ruffians, poking fun and making light of what was going on in the service. One night he had actually stormed into the church and grabbed his sister, pulling her up from her knees, throwing her across his shoulder, pushing his way through the crowd, and depositing her outside. In front of his cheering friends, he warned his sister never to go back to the altar again. A few days later he was dead, a victim of a bolt of lightning.

I learned then the meaning of Isaiah 57:15–16:

> For thus saith the high and lofty One that inhabiteth eternity, whose name is Holy; I dwell in the high and holy place, with him also that is of a contrite and humble spirit, to revive the spirit of the humble, and to revive the heart of the contrite ones. For I will not contend for ever.

Looking back on those early revivals, I realize now that those experiences were as much for my own benefit as they were for the people to whom I preached my heart out. God was teaching me—this was my training ground, my college, my seminary. He wanted me to trust Him completely and to learn to take authority over the power of the devil. I received my instructions from the Word of God. I looked at the life of David, for instance, and saw clearly that this young man killed the bear and the lion before he ever faced the giant. God was showing me that if He could bring revival to an entire community, this same power could shake great cities, and even entire nations. The power and the anointing of the Holy Spirit I felt when I preached in little towns throughout the southern part of the United States was the same anointing I would later experience when I preached to thousands of souls in the great outdoor crusades in Manila. It is this same anointing that today enables me to minister daily to millions by way of radio, television, and the printed page.

And so the lesson was learned, never to be forgotten: Genuine revival comes when God's people use the authority He has given them. When we become God's children, the blood of Jesus Christ and the Book become our authority. Jesus taught this authority in Matthew 18:18: "Whatsoever ye shall bind on earth shall be bound in heaven: and whatsoever ye shall loose on earth shall be loosed in heaven."

I could still get discouraged, though. One time I was visiting my brother who pastored a church in Tennessee. I was staying in his home and preaching twenty miles out in the country. My brother said to his wife, "Go and listen to Lester preach. See what he can do."

Following the service that she attended, I overheard, through the ventilator into the bedroom where I slept, this conversation:

"Honey, how did Lester do?"

"Oh, Bud," she replied, "he wouldn't make a preacher in a thousand years!"

At first I was indignant. For one thing, I didn't intend to be around a thousand years! But then I was hurt. It looked as though I'd never make it out of the brush-arbor circuit. And I began to cry. I was heartbroken, and I prostrated myself on the floor in that bedroom. Depression seemed to be settling in like a heavy, blanketing fog; but late in the evening, around midnight, God spoke to me—God has spoken to me in every crisis of my life through His Word. I reached for my Bible and read Luke 4:18:

> The Spirit of the Lord is upon me, because he hath anointed me to preach the gospel to the poor; he hath sent me to heal the broken-hearted, to preach deliverance to the captives, and recovering of sight to the blind, to set at liberty them that are bruised.

I jumped up and thought, "Hey! *The Spirit of the Lord is upon me.*" That made me feel good. "Well, if the Spirit of the Lord is upon me, evidently I'm going to do something. *He has anointed me.*" I studied the verse carefully. I knew I was finding more direction for my life. This was my destiny. It was no small affair. No man's destiny is a small affair in the sight of Almighty God.

Even though my brother and his wife, both of whom I loved and respected, thought I wouldn't make it in preaching in a thousand years, maybe, just maybe God was going to do something special with me that had nothing to do with natural talent.

At one point as I studied Jesus' words, I felt His gentle rebuke. Remember, I was young; and though I was gaining in experience, I still had a lot to learn. When I read, "He hath anointed me to preach the gospel to the poor," I thought, "Hey, wait a minute, God. I haven't gotten into preaching just to preach to the down-and-outers for the rest of my life. I may be preaching to farmers now, but—" and as I carried on that conversation in my head with the Lord, it was as though I heard Him say, "Lester, that's not the poor I'm talking about. Everyone who hasn't heard My

31

message is poor. Everyone who doesn't understand the mighty power of the Holy Spirit is poor. Those in the heathen lands who have never heard My name, they are *very* poor."

Slowly, the picture began to emerge. God's plan began to unfold in my mind's eye. I started asking God questions. "I can understand about healing the brokenhearted. I know what it feels like to be brokenhearted. I think I can help those who are hurting. And preaching deliverance—I've seen people already who have been delivered from the bonds of Satan. But recovering of sight to the blind and setting at liberty them that are bruised—what does all that mean, Lord?"

"Those who don't know Me, they are the ones who are truly blind. When they receive knowledge of Me, then their eyes are opened. Those who are hurting, who've been bruised by the devil time after time, they need to be set at liberty. Lester, you can do it through Me."

God lifted me up off the bedroom floor that night, and while I didn't have a blueprint giving me all the directions I needed, I knew there was work out there for me to do and I'd better move on. I had been chosen and anointed, and it was just a matter of God's timing before I was sent to preach to the multitudes of the world.

5

At the Appointed Time

On December 18, 1931, the night of my second and last vision, far away in London, England, Howard Carter was praying. God spoke to this former inventor, son of an inventor, theologian, and Hampstead Bible Institute president. He was so moved by what he sensed God was telling him that he wrote the words of the message down:

I have found a companion for thee; I have called a worker to stand beside thee. He hath heard my call, he respondeth, he joineth thee in the work to which I have called thee. I have called him, although thou hast not seen him. He is called and chosen and shalt join thee. Behold he cometh; he cometh from afar. He cometh to help thee to carry thy burden and be a strength at thy side, and thou shalt find pleasure in his service and shalt delight in his fellowship. He shalt come at the time appointed and shalt not tarry; at a time thou thinkest not shalt he appear, even when thou art engaged in my work.

Carter read that to his Bible institute teachers. Since he

wasn't a married man, at first his co-workers thought it meant he would be meeting and marrying a pretty woman in some other country. But Carter set them straight. The prophecy hadn't said anything about a woman; in fact, the personal pronoun reference all the way through had been "he."

Eighteen months after that, this great man of God came to America. I'd never heard of him. He'd never heard of me. By this time I was preaching in Oklahoma, and in that way whereby I know when God is telling me to do something, I sensed that I was to go to Eureka Springs, Arkansas. I knew of the tri-state camp meeting being held there and felt certain that it was God's will for me to attend.

I closed out my revival meeting, and my sister and I drove one hundred fifty miles to Eureka Springs. We left with objections of the local pastor ringing in our ears, but I felt compelled to go.

Upon arriving, Leona and I went to a teaching service where Howard Carter was speaking. When he was finished, he went outside and so did I. I walked up, shook his hand, introduced myself, and said: "Thank you for the Word of God." Then I heard myself saying some very strange things: "You know, I'll go with you wherever you go. I'll help you. I'll try to strengthen you. It would be a pleasure and a delight to fellowship with you."

Years later, in an article that appeared in our *World Harvest* magazine, Howard Carter told of that encounter:

> His words excited me. He was repeating the message God had given me in London. . . . When I heard the very words of the Lord's message to me flowing from his lips, I was immediately convinced that a miracle was taking

place . . . the matter certainly amazed me; and I said within myself that this young man was, without doubt, the one of whom the Lord had spoken in 1931.

Howard Carter asked me to come with him; he said he had something he wanted to show me. Another gentleman accompanied us; and when we got to Carter's hotel room, he pulled out a little black book. Then he and the man went to one corner of the room, and Carter showed him the book. I could hear "Oh" from first one and then the other.

When they came back to me, Carter explained. "Young man, it seems that God has done something very unusual today."

Now it was my turn to say "Oh."

"What do you do?" he asked.

"I'm an evangelist," I replied.

"Do you have any intention of being a missionary?" he questioned.

"I'm on my way around the world right now!" I quickly replied.

"You are!" His voice showed his delight and surprise. Then he added, "How long have you known that you were supposed to go around the world?"

"For eighteen months. Ever since I had a vision of the world going to hell." Then I told him about my vision.

Carter had me sit down. "I want to show you something, Lester," he said. "God gave me a prophecy eighteen months ago. It appears that it was at the same time He gave you your vision. Here, read this. I wrote it down immediately afterward."

I took the black book, and there I read "He is called and

chosen." Can you imagine how overwhelmed I was at that moment?

Sensing my amazement, Carter said, "The very words you spoke to me outside there on the sidewalk." He began to explain to me about the nine gifts of the Spirit and that the "word of wisdom" was one such gift. I had not walked into Howard Carter's life by mere chance.

"Are you willing to travel with me?" he asked.

"I'm ready to go," I fairly shouted. We shook hands and parted company.

Leona and I started driving to Mobile, Alabama, where our family had moved since I started preaching. On the way, as I was telling Leona all about the conversation with Howard Carter, I remembered that I hadn't even given him an address where I could be reached. I knew he was on his way to the West Coast, and from there he would begin his journey around the world. So I lost him. In the same hour when he found me and I found him, we lost each other.

But I had a beautiful peace. "Leona," I said, "I'm going to sell my car, get a passport, and then get a ticket to California, and I'll catch up with Howard Carter." When we reached our parents' home and they learned of my plans, my father *really* thought I was out of my mind. Imagine thinking you could start off on an around-the-world trip to preach the gospel when you barely had enough money to get to California!

6

To the Bottom of the World

The Los Angeles of the thirties was not nearly as large as the Los Angeles of today. But for a down-to-earth country boy like me, it loomed mighty big. I stepped down off that train and pulled out of my pocket the slip of paper that told me where Bethel Temple and Dr. Turnbull were. Upon arriving at this church, I introduced myself. "I'm Lester Sumrall, an evangelist."

"Yes, I know," Dr. Turnbull replied with a smile. "Howard Carter spoke about you. He said you would preach for me."

"Where is Howard Carter?" I asked.

"I think he's in Japan," he answered.

To myself I mused: "Hmm, Japan. That's about a 100 million people. But I'll find him."

Arthur Protcham, pastor of a church in Manhattan Beach, had invited me over to preach for him. I asked him if he knew Howard Carter. "Oh, yes," he said. "We're bosom buddies from way back. We're both Englishmen from London."

"Do you know where he is?"

"In China."

China had 500 million people. That totaled 600 million (with Japan) among whom I'd have to search for one man.

In Manhattan Beach I met a very close friend of Howard Carter, Dr. Lillian Yeomans, a much-respected medical doctor. She said, "Come over for dinner." What a remarkable woman she turned out to be!

Before dinner she invited me to kneel on what she called her prayer carpet. "Kneel on that," she directed. "God's Holy Ghost is in it!"

She laughed and I laughed. I was from the hills of Arkansas, the plains of Oklahoma, the tall timber of Mississippi, and from Alabama and Florida. That's pretty down home. I'd never knelt on a carpet like that. But down I went, and I'm glad I did. My, could that lady pray! "Lord, I can't be a missionary now. You know I'm eighty-five. But this young man can go. Let him have the faith that is in my heart. Let him have the impetus and vitality that is in my soul. Send him forth just as if I were going." I really sensed the power of God flood over my being as Dr. Yeomans prayed that life-changing prayer.

Then I asked her if she knew where Howard Carter was. "India!" she said without batting an eyelash.

Japan. China. India. "Dear God," I said, "that's another 500 hundred million! I'm not sure now that I can *ever* find him!"

Deep inside I heard, "Pray about it."

So I prayed. "Lord, how am I going to find this man?"

"Of course you know," He answered. "Go to the bottom." God has some unusual ways of getting His message through.

"Go to the bottom!" I repeated it with more than a little incredulity. I wasn't meaning to sound skeptical, but I might· have. The truth of the matter was that I was genuinely surprised. "What's the bottom?" I heard myself say.

And then I heard, "Australia."

From southern California it was on up to San Francisco on my journey around the world. I was the guest of a Dr. Craig of the Glad Tidings Temple and Bible School. Even though I preached in his large auditorium to big audiences for three nights, and even though I accompanied some of his students out for street witnessing, I hadn't received any money. But he did offer to drive me to the dock to board the boat for Australia.

"Young man, it must be wonderful to be rich and young, on your way to travel around the world," he said to me.

I didn't realize he was referring to me, so I said, "Yes, I think that would be great."

"You do have sufficient funds to return home without any trouble, don't you?"

"God knows what I have," I said, "and He knows what I need."

"I believe," he continued, "that you should make an itemized list of your proposed expenses to determine whether you really can afford to make this trip."

"That's not necessary," I said, "because I need everything. I don't have anything."

At that point he became very concerned. "Young man, you may get stranded someplace and starve."

"Well, if I do, Dr. Craig, just send over a little tombstone that reads: 'Here lies Lester Sumrall, who starved to death trusting Jesus'!"

He was shocked and may have been somewhat hurt by my attitude and youthful brashness, but that's the way I left the shores of this country on my first overseas trip.

The day I started around the world, I wept. I had just turned twenty and had been on the road preaching since leaving home. I'd left home with meager belongings and a raging father shouting after me, "You'll starve," while my precious mother, hands crossed over her breast and tears rolling down her cheeks, was silently praying. I remember now, as clearly as though it happened yesterday, the feeling that swept over me as I stood on the deck of the R.M.S. *Makura* as it steamed through the deep water channel past infamous Alcatraz and under the Golden Gate Bridge off the harbor of San Francisco. I'd stuck my hand in my pocket, and there I felt my wallet. The realization swept over me then that all the money I had in the world was right there. Twelve dollars.

Tears trickled down my cheeks. I was still just a young man, and I felt pretty much alone. At that moment, without visible friends and with no financial backing, I leaned heavily on the Lord. Earlier I knew He had told me where I was to go and what I was to do. Now I needed to hear His voice again. I shut out the sounds all around me—the hundreds of other passengers lining the ship's railing, the boat's whistle, the sounds coming from deep below deck in the belly of the ship—and I just stood there, silently repeating the words of John 15:16 to myself: "Ye have not chosen me, but I have chosen you."

What a trip it turned out to be! Paul's thorn was also

with me, a "messenger of Satan [sent] to buffet" (2 Cor. 12:7), in the person of a young Austrian infidel who tried to tear me to shreds with his angry tongue. As I walked on deck, he would announce my approach to all within hearing distance by saying, "Here comes that funny fellow who believes in a red devil with a long pointed tail and pitchfork!" At the dinner table he would mockingly say, "Everybody be quiet now, the preacher is going to pray for us all!"

After days of this kind of ridicule, the Lord told me to take him aside and tell him about my healing from tuberculosis. I did, and the mocking stopped.

Some Anglicans on board didn't understand what a young faith preacher was doing on a ship bound for Australia, and they also tried to make things difficult. The devil gave it to me for twenty-one days in one way or another. But this was a part of my schooling, a necessary experience that would better equip me for what lay ahead.

After traveling 4,200 miles and crossing the equator, we stopped at the French town of Papeete on the island of Tahiti, the "Paradise of the Pacific." I was charmed immediately by the pearl divers in the lagoons, the palm trees nodding over the coral beaches, the thatch-roofed huts with woven-grass panel walls, and the colorful garb of the bronze-skinned Polynesians. But on closer look, I discovered the debauchery of this world-famous international playground.

I found myself praying about what I was observing. In my heart I knew the Lord was telling me that this was typical of the condition of the world. "Preach to them. Pour out your heart to them," He was saying.

From Tahiti we resumed our journey and next touched

shore at Avarua on the British-owned island of Rarotonga in the Cook island chain. On this island sin did not appear to be as flagrant; still, I sensed the need was there, too.

Eighteen hundred miles farther southwest we spotted the snow-topped mountains of the North Island of New Zealand. We entered Cook Strait and finally docked at Port Nicholson near Wellington, the capital city, in an area that experiences over a hundred earthquakes a year.

I was weary of travel. I was only too glad to be able to get off the boat. To myself I wondered: "Where should I begin my search for Howard Carter?" We were to have a thirty-six-hour stopover in Wellington. I could not know that even as I left that steamer and walked down the gangplank, Howard Carter was in the mountainous interior of New Zealand, teaching at a minister's retreat.

While praying, Howard Carter had asked God, "Where is the young man who was supposed to meet me in California? God, I've lost track of him."

The Spirit of God spoke to his heart: "That traveling companion is not lost. He is in Wellington and will be going to churches there seeking your whereabouts. Send the Wellington pastor home with a note for Lester Sumrall."

I didn't know what awaited me as I disembarked, but one thing I felt for sure—God wasn't going to let me get stranded someplace and starve.

I trudged up and down the hills of Wellington in the middle of their summer, which is December, in my winter clothes, searching for a Full-Gospel church. Inquiring at a large Anglican cathedral in the center of town brought no information. I'd found Baptist, Methodist, and Presbyterian churches. I'd located the Salvation Army. Finally, I stopped a man on the street and asked, "Is there any church in this town where the people say 'Hallelujah' or 'Praise the Lord'?"

He laughed and said, "Yes, I think so," and pointed across the railroad tracks out of town. "Go out that street and up a little hill and you'll find it."

I followed his directions, crossed the tracks, and climbed the hill. Then I spotted it—a lovely little, white church. Next to it was a charming little house that I assumed correctly to be the parsonage. While I was walking toward the door, the Wellington pastor and his wife were inside, waiting and wondering if someone were really going to show up. Howard Carter had given them a card to hand to someone by the name of Lester Sumrall. Carter had assured the Wellington pastor that the Holy Spirit had told him this young man would be in Wellington searching for him.

I knocked and the pastor opened the door. "Yes?" His voice boomed. He was a giant of a man. That voice would almost knock a timid person off the porch!

"You don't know who I am, but—"

He interrupted, "Yes, I do know who you are. You're Lester Sumrall."

I was so stunned that I nearly fainted. "Come in, Brother, come in," the man with the big voice was saying. "Here's something from Howard Carter for you." He handed me the card.

"Mr. Sumrall," the card read, "continue on to Australia and minister there. I will meet you in Sydney." It was signed by Howard Carter.

This was my second encounter with one of the functions of the gifts of the Holy Spirit. I enjoyed the fellowship with this Wellington pastor and his wife, and when my thirty-six-hour stopover in New Zealand came to an end, I again boarded the steamship for the two day's journey on to Australia.

At 4:30 in the morning two days later, I awoke and peered out the porthole at the glimmering lights of Sydney Harbor. Later I was to realize that this is one of the world's most beautiful natural harbors.

Before we were allowed to disembark, the Australian immigration authorities issued declaration forms to all passengers. One question read: "How much money do you have with you?" In small print it said: "Foreigners planning to stay in Australia three months or longer are required to have with them not less than two hundred pounds or the equivalent."

Of course I had to leave the space blank. As I stood in line waiting my turn, a young American in front of me was refused entry because he had only seventy-five dollars.

Momentarily, I trembled and the thought flashed through my mind: "Surely God wouldn't let me come all this way only to be refused entry!" The officer was asking for my declaration form, and I jumped.

"An American, eh?" he said. "Sir, you've left a question unanswered. How much money do you have on you?" His pen was poised in midair, ready to write down my reply.

"I don't have much money," I said.

"Hmm," he said, stroking his chin. "You're a minister. Where do you plan to go from here?"

"I'm en route around the world to preach," I answered. "I hope to go on to Java, China, Korea, Manchuria, Japan, then to Europe, and back to America." (I was surprised at my audacity as I replied promptly.) "God has called me to preach the gospel all over the world to people who don't know Christ as Savior. God is sending me, and I know that He will provide for all my needs."

The officer stared at me for a moment, then murmured, "Excuse me a minute." He walked away to the chief inspector while I prayed silently.

The inspector asked the same question, and I replied in a similar manner. The two men then had a short conference while I continued my own short, private conference with the Lord. The next thing I knew, the inspector was back, saying, "We are going to allow you to land."

I collected my baggage and disembarked with great rejoicing in my heart. From the dock I made my way to the railroad station for the six-hundred-mile trip south to Melbourne. I was met there by a Mr. Greenwood, pastor of Richmond Temple, who had invited me to speak at his church. My diary reveals that we traveled by motor car through what seemed to be millions of grasshoppers crunching and beating against the windshield, roof, and sides of the car. Such was my introduction to the "land down under."

Traveling through the southwest corner of the province of New South Wales, we skirted the gorgeous Snowy Mountains, passed ancient gold and copper mines, cattle and sheep stations, twenty-foot-high ant hills, and occasionally saw a loping kangaroo. But mostly my eyes were fixed on the people. It was to be the first foreign country for me to preach in, and I was studying the faces of the people.

Melbourne, the former capital city of Australia, claims one-sixth of the total population of the entire continent. I had been told that there were seven thousand acres of parks and gardens. My eyes were fixed on the long rows of English look-alike houses. I stayed with a family from the church in the middle of what was to me a very confusing block of homes. After I had preached for a week, the pastor thanked me profusely. But again I was confronted with the comment, "It must be wonderful to be rich like you Americans."

Back in my room I vented my desperation. I reminded God that I was scheduled to go to Bendigo, a city about a hundred miles away, and that I had no money for a ticket. I determined that I wouldn't leave the room and go out on the sidewalk with my suitcase without a ticket. I laid on the floor and cried out to God, asking Him to take care of my needs.

I awakened in the morning to the sound of a gentle tap on the door. "Brother Sumrall, breakfast is ready," my hostess said. I thanked her and said I wouldn't be eating. I busied myself packing and put my suitcase, briefcase, and Bible by the door. I heard the man of the house leave for work, and about an hour later there was another knock on my door. "Brother Sumrall," my hostess said, "there's a man to see you from the church. Would you see him?"

This big, fine-looking Australian came into the room, and I could tell he'd been weeping. "I couldn't sleep last night," he said.

"Neither could I," I told him.

"Now, if this isn't right," he said, "I won't ever try it again."

"What are you talking about?" I asked.

"Well, I know you Americans are rich, but I know you are supposed to go to Bendigo to preach, and I didn't know if you knew you needed a reservation to get on the train going there. It's a 'Special,' and you can't get on without an advance reservation."

I interrupted him to say, "I didn't know that."

He looked relieved and continued, "Well, I felt God told me that—that you didn't realize this—so I went down and purchased the ticket for you. And I'm honored, Sir, to be able to present it to you."

That Australian was one happy man. He almost danced in the street as we left that house and made our way to the train station. And I've been telling people for a long time that when God tells you something, you'd better believe Him. If that young man hadn't listened—regardless of how strange it seemed to him—I might have been stranded in Melbourne, and that San Francisco pastor's prophecy could have come true. When we parted those many years ago, we promised each other that we'd be faithful to what the Lord tells us, and we'd meet in heaven and laugh about it and praise the Lord together some more.

7

From Evangelist to Missionary

"When you evangelists come from America, all you want is to minister in our larger churches. Why don't you raise up a church?" After the meetings in Bendigo, I was challenged with those words to pioneer a new church in Brisbane, capital city of Queensland. The person saying them was challenging the right man, since that fit perfectly with the vision I felt God had given me. I rented a tent, distributed handbills, and found that hungry hearts in the land down under were no different from hungry hearts in America.

God can make a missionary when He wants to. I was no longer the "white" young preacher from Florida. I now felt a little of what Abraham of the Old Testament may have felt. I don't think that old-time father of faith ever bothered worrying about whether he had enough faith to go around. His walk of faith was natural. So, too, was mine. I knew I was doing the thing I was supposed to do, that I was where God wanted me to be. My experiences were faith-building ones that would stand me in good stead for the rest of my life.

The first tent church we pitched in Australia was right across the street from a pub (which is another word for a tavern). The Australians liked to go there, socialize, and drink. The tent audience thought nothing of it when drunks would amble into our meetings, calling me names and disturbing the singing and preaching. They laughed at my accent and my being an American. When I asked the volunteer ushers to throw them out, they said, "Why? They aren't hurting you." There was only one thing left to do—exercise some authority. So I took it upon myself to boot them out of the tent. My Irish temperament helped considerably.

After that the congregation gave me a five-minute standing ovation, and the next night over four hundred people turned out to hear the American evangelist.

Communist agitators heckled us some nights. Whenever I mentioned world conditions or Russia, they went wild. One night they were especially unruly; so I shouted to the congregation, "When you talk about the devil, his children get angry!" That was the last we saw of them.

I learned from those experiences not to take the enemy's assaults sitting down. My faith in a God who was mightier than any of the devil's followers was powerful. I began to understand 2 Corinthians 10:4–5:

For the weapons of our warfare are not physical (weapons of flesh and blood), but they are mighty before God for the overthrow and destruction of strongholds, [Inasmuch as we] refute arguments and theories and reasonings and every proud and lofty thing that sets itself up against the (true) knowledge of God (Amp. Bible).

Signs and miracles followed the preaching of God's Word in the "Gospel Tabernacle" tent, and at the end of six weeks there was a congregation of about three hundred converts. They found a pastor, and a church was established there that continues to this day.

The time had now come for me to meet Howard Carter once again in the port of Sydney. It had been five months since we had first met, and we embraced with hearts full of joy in anticipation of what lay ahead. It was January 1, 1935, when he stepped off the beautiful, white S.S. Maraposa and we began our missionary venture together.

In the next two months, we traveled throughout Australia wherever God opened doors. Sometimes we ministered together; at other times we ministered in different places. One of the blessings of this ministry occurred in the establishment of a Bible school in Queensland for the preparation of young Australians for the ministry.

Carter's presence was so unassuming that it was easy to miss his greatness. In him I observed a smooth-flowing, simple faith and a life that demonstrated the quiet trust he had in the Lord. He became my spiritual father, more of a father to me than my own dad. He influenced my ministry perhaps more than any other man. I could preach the poorest sermons, and he would say, "You know, Mr. Sumrall, that's a very fine sermon. I can give you a few little pointers, if you'd like, for the next time you preach it." I was just twenty-one years old and he was forty-one. I needed his tutoring and the inspiration he provided. Together we moved out in faith. If I needed a shirt, he'd get it for me. We had no guaranteed stipend, but God always provided.

On March 9, the gangplank was lifted and a harbor tugboat gently pulled the S.S. *Morella* away from her moorings. We stood on deck and waved farewell to our Australian brothers and sisters whom we had come to love. We sensed their great love, too, as we heard the words of the song "God Be with You 'til We Meet Again." Our destination was Java, Indonesia, a fifteen-day journey.

As we settled in on ship, we noted our surroundings. The S.S. *Morella* was formerly the privately owned pleasure yacht of Germany's Kaiser Wilhelm II before his abdication and self-imposed exile to the Netherlands in 1918. The seagoing luxury hotel had been confiscated by Great Britain as war booty after World War I and was being used for shuttle service through the Coral Sea between Brisbane and the island of Java.

It was among gorgeous tapestries, marble columns, painted ceilings, gold and white mirrors, and by the enormous, white, fresh-water pool that Howard Carter and I really got acquainted. I began to learn more about this refined Englishman's background, and he learned about this brash, young American. We laughed together, studied the Word of God, and prayed. This was a necessary time together before launching out into the wide mission fields of the world. I came to look upon him as an Elijah. He, in turn, regarded me as his Elisha.

8

Into Training with God

Java, one of the Spice Islands of Indonesia, comprises a string of high, barren, volcanic cones and low, fertile plains. It was on this torrid, humid island of perpetual summer that I felt I was getting the kind of training, with God as my teacher, that would stand me in good stead for the rest of my life. For three years the apostle Paul had his course in the university of Arabia, a wilderness training to be sure (see Gal. 1:15–18). I felt I received mine among these islanders.

Dr. S. D. Gordon has written:

God is anxious that His children get a good education. Every man He has used has had a course in the university of Arabia, a wilderness training. Joseph, Moses, Elijah, John the Herald, Paul, Bunyan, Morrison, Judson, even the divine Son Himself in the days of His humanity— these are a few of the distinguished graduates. But the fees are large, the course severely high, the discipline exacting, and many don't keep it up but drop out. The marked results are broad perspective, steady nerves, keen eyesight and insight. There come utter dependence on God, utter independence of man, childlike simplicity, warm sympathy, and deep humility. But the highest degree goes to patience, the rarest trait of all, most God-like, hardest and longest to acquire. God has no short-cuts in His training.

I would not have you think that I am comparing myself to the apostle Paul, but I am relating the facts concerning my own personal school of training that I believe was God-ordained as preparatory evangelization work to equip me for the years ahead.

There were 45 million people, most of whom were farm people in 1935, living in small villages when we reached the 666-mile equatorial island-paradise lying between the Indian Ocean and the Java Sea. We were only going to be there for three months, but we had so many invitations at times that I thought we could stay there the rest of our lives. We preached our hearts out day after day, night after night, each in different places in order to cover more territory.

Our ship, the S.S. *Morella*, docked at the East Indian port of Surabaja, where we were met by Mr. and Mrs. Van Abkonde, who were to be our hosts. Immediately I was enchanted by the pearl divers and half-clad coolies. I quickly discerned that Java was a land of contrasts. The Van Abkondes took us to their home in Temanggoeng, which became a sort of base as we traveled from city to city, from village to village crisscrossing the island. We preached, it seemed, to everything that had breath between the Royal Chop Block at the Sultan's palace in Djokjakarta to a bamboo tabernacle with an earthen floor in the mountain village of Gambang Walla.

So hungry for the truth were these people that at our first meeting, in a large, concrete auditorium designed to seat twelve hundred people, there were over two thousand people present with hundreds standing in the aisles and around the wall. It was thrilling to hear the Javanese choir sing the "Hallelujah Chorus." While we had to speak through an interpreter, "Hallelujah" was the one word of their language we understood.

When I looked out over that vast, cosmopolitan audience, I saw familiar faces. There were Malaysians, Javanese, Dutch, Chinese, and English faces. I was amazed at how familiar they appeared to me. *Where had I seen them?* And just that quickly I knew. It was the vision! Yes, I had seen them in the vision! Later, when the invitation was given and great numbers came forward to receive salvation, as I saw all these different races kneeling at the altar, praying to one God, I saw once again that the ground was level at Calvary. All are equally welcome at the cross.

I was so young then and not familiar with all the old hymns. But years later I was to hear the words "In Christ there is no East nor West, in Him no South or North, But one great fellowship of Love, throughout the whole wide earth" ("In Christ There Is No East or West," *Hymns of Praise*, Hope Pub.), and I recalled that meeting.

Java had for centuries been a nation of Buddhists, Hindus, and Muslims. There were demon worshipers among the islanders. We found over seventy regional dialects, though there was one official Indonesian language. For the most part, the light-brown-skinned women, with straight black hair, dressed in brilliantly colored, long, side-slit skirts, with small turbans on their heads. The men

54

wore short, white coats over their trousers. Both wore sandals. This picturesque garb was pleasing. But we learned that women were held in such low esteem that, if a man lost his wife, his neighbor might give him one of his at no charge. How much they needed to hear about Jesus' love for *all* people and to see how He treated women.

Every evening on the streets we saw the traditional Javanese shadow shows, like marionettes behind a flat drape, depicting events from their remote past. Much of this centered on highly unrealistic, grotesque gods and ancient tribal rituals. There were dramatic folk dances representing scenes of adventure, battle, and love. The audience was often laughing uproariously as the weaker hero prevailed over the stronger villain.

In the suffocating humidity we rode buses and trains packed to over-capacity with people who piled their suit-cases, garden produce, and poultry high in the seats and aisles. Their mouths were blood-red from chewing a mixture of tobacco and a drug called *menjan*. From paneless windows we watched natives working in terraced rice pad-dies on the sides of volcanic mountains, a scene we were to see over and over throughout our travels in the Orient. Plowmen rode astride their water buffalo or ambled be-hind, guiding the primitive wooden plow. We visited cacao plantations and local native markets, musical with loudly clacking abacuses. We feasted on rice/meat/hot pepper dishes, tropical fruit, and aged duck eggs, while bamboo-shoot-chewing monkeys peered at us from be-hind banana trees or played alongside the roads.

It was a cultural shock, to be sure, and this country boy from the Deep South did a lot of neck-craning. There were times when I longed to sink my teeth into some of

Mother's good cookin'—some country ham, grits, or hot biscuits—but on the whole, it was a pleasant experience. The main problem we encountered was what I refer to as "the curse of Babel," the language barrier. This was to prove true in most of the countries I visited in the years ahead.

It was on this island that I was first confronted with a demon-possessed person. At one of the services a girl, eleven or twelve years old, with wild eyes, approached the platform, sank to the floor, and began writhing like a snake. Her tongue would dart in and out of her mouth in quick little jabs. It was frightening, yet no one paid any attention to her. I got the impression that this had happened before. But it was new to me. Meanwhile, the service continued as though nothing was going on at the front of the platform.

When the song service was over, the prayer was prayed, the Scripture was read, and the announcements were given, we were already forty-five minutes into the service; and the pastors looked across at me, signaling that it was my turn to begin the message. I looked down at the girl once again and saw a stream of green foam oozing from her mouth. I sent a telegram prayer to the Lord urging Him to hurry up and do something about the girl. But nothing happened.

As I approached the pulpit, I prayed silently, "God, save souls here tonight." And then in that way I have come to recognize as God speaking, I heard, "Take care of the girl first."

Immediately I responded with "Oh, no, God. You take care of her. I don't know what to do!"

"Lester, you're in charge. It's your responsibility."

God continued speaking to my inner man. This was a new kind of problem to me. I'd never faced demon-possession before, never had heard a sermon on the subject, and had never read a book about it. But I knew there was something in this girl that needed to come out of her. A divine urgency was building up in me. Usually when I first approach a new audience, I will give a greeting: "I'm so glad to be on your beautiful island, etc., etc." But that's not what I said this time. Instead, I pointed over the pulpit at the girl still writhing on the floor and shouted in English, "Get up and sit down!"

The startled interpreter gawked at me in surprise. That wasn't what he expected! The girl, of course, understood no English, but the demon understood. The girl took her hand and wiped the green mess off her face, backed up to the first pew, and sat down like a zombie. She sat as motionless as a statue for forty-five minutes as I preached.

When I finished my sermon, instead of giving an altar call, without premeditation I looked at the girl and commanded the demonic spirits, "Now come out of her!"

Immediately that transfixed look left her face. Her rigid body relaxed. She smiled, blinked her eyes, and her whole countenance changed. She became a pretty little girl before our eyes. When the audience realized that this child had been set free, hundreds came running down the aisles to be freed themselves by this same power of God. It brought a tremendous victory into the meeting as scores of souls received Christ as their Savior.

Howard Carter was ministering in another place that night, but when we both got back to our room, I told him about what took place. I finished by saying, "I hope that never happens again!" I told him I felt like a spiritual surgeon, and I really didn't relish any more such encounters. He related to me some of his own encounters with possessed people and told me I shouldn't be surprised when we encountered demonic power. In Indonesia there were more witch doctors than medical doctors, and curses of black magic were an everyday fact in almost every village.

It was just a week later, in a different town, when I had another unnerving experience. Again the mission hall was packed to capacity. Extra chairs had been brought in, and still people had to stand. The hunger in the hearts of these people was plainly evident. That night as I entered and began to walk down the crowded aisle, a woman grabbed my coat and wouldn't let go. I didn't know whether to try to jerk loose from the woman or try something else. I finally set my Bible case on the floor and leaned over to pry her fingers loose. She glared into my face with snake eyes, grinned evily, and spoke to me in English: "There's a black angel in you, and there's a white angel in me!"

I placed my hands on the sides of her head and said, "That's a lie. I have the Spirit of Jesus Christ in me, and you have the devil in you with the blackness of hell." Then, addressing the demonic spirit in her, I spoke firmly, "In the name of Jesus, I command you to come out of her."

Her eyes changed. Her face relaxed. She was released! I touched her gently, my hand on her shoulder, and through the interpreter asked, "How long have you been like that?"

The woman calmly replied, "Fifteen years ago I went to a witch doctor, and the evil spirit has been in me from that day to this. But I know I am free of it now." And she looked up at me with a sweet smile on what had only moments before been an angry, contorted face.

The glory of God spread through the audience. As I continued walking among them, I was able to minister to many others, my friend interpreting as we moved through the crowd.

Later, in talking about this with Howard Carter, I was able to put it in perspective with his help. "Any time someone is set free, that's good!" he said. "It doesn't matter how it happens, whether you are in the pulpit or walking through the crowd. The way to score a spiritual victory is to face whatever it is when it happens. Sometimes you don't even have time to think what the battle strategy should be. You just have to be prepared, prayed up, and willing to do battle. The Word of God is your sword. When those people saw that you weren't afraid of the devil, it brought faith and victory to the entire assembly. I don't think this is the end of your battles with demons, Mr. Sumrall."

I knew the Bible had plenty to say on the subject of doing battle with the adversary; so, Bible in hand, I retreated to search out the teachings that would better equip me for what lay ahead. Ephesians 6:11–18 shows that our life is going to be a warfare:

> Put on the whole armor of God, that ye may be able to stand against the wiles of the devil. For we wrestle not against flesh and blood, but against principalities, against powers, against the rulers of the darkness of this world, against spiritual wickedness in high places. Wherefore take unto you the whole armor of God, that ye may be able to withstand in the evil day, and having done all, to stand. Stand therefore, having your loins girt about with truth, and having on the breastplate of righteousness; And your feet shod with the preparation of the gospel of peace;

Above all, taking the shield of faith, wherewith ye shall be able to quench all the fiery darts of the wicked. And take the helmet of salvation, and the sword of the Spirit, which is the word of God: Praying always with all prayer and supplication in the Spirit, and watching thereunto with all perseverance and supplication for all saints.

In all my travels since, I have not seen as much demonic power as I saw demonstrated in Java. The Javanese reverence their witch doctors. Whenever one boards a bus or train, the passengers give him gifts. Buses stop in villages to let the witch doctor "bless" the people.

The greatest thing I learned was that it was not me personally in conflict with demonic power, nor was it the possessed person with whom I battled. It was always the devils within them. I learned also that there was no reason to fear, because God never loses a battle. In other encounters I saw possessed people tearing at themselves, hurting themselves in the process; but in most cases, the demons didn't want to touch or harm *me*. Howard Carter was instrumental in pointing me to those passages in the Bible that showed Jesus' casting out demons and telling the disciples that they should do likewise (see Mark 16:15–17).

I saw God sovereign in His control of the affairs of men and nations and magnificent in His glory. It was awesome for this young man from the southern part of the United States. I think back to the day a Dutch banker invited Mr. Carter and I to see the live crater of Merapi, one of many active volcanos at that time, which had erupted several years previously. We had to climb the serpentine trail on horseback, but once on top, the sulphuric earth at the crest of the mountain was "alive" and almost cooked our shoe leather. As we peered over the edge, the boiling lava leaping up like liquid hell and the stench of almost over-powering sulphur fumes reminded me of the vision I had seen of the world on its way to hell.

I crawled on my knees to the tip of a grassy ledge and gazed down for a time, fascinated by the movement in the black cauldron, not noticing that the ground beneath me had been eaten away. Suddenly, the earth dropped and I felt myself falling toward the bubbling lava two hundred feet below. The banker, with lightning speed, grabbed my shirt and, with superhuman strength, sent me flying backward over the top of his head. We both went sprawling on the grass twenty feet from the rim, where there was now a gaping hole. What a testimony this was to the three of us to the watchcare of the Lord over those whom He loves.

Without exaggeration, I can say that we preached the gospel of Christ to as many as we possibly could while we were there. We preached to those in the American con-sul, in the Javanese magistrates, in beautiful Full-Gospel churches, in hired Masonic auditoriums and movie houses, in the bamboo huts of the humblest peasants in villages hidden away in the mountainous regions. In those three months, according to Brother Carter's meticulous record-keeping, we covered more than three thousand miles and preached in about a hundred different cities, towns, and villages with strange-sounding names— Blabok, Semarang, Surakarta, Probolinggo, Magelang, Kediri, and Tjilatjap, to name just a few.

But then it was time to move on.

9

Where East Meets West

From Java we sailed to the flat, swampy island of Singapore and into the port city of Singapore itself, considered to be one of the world's busiest ports and the major commercial and shipping center of Southeast Asia. It is a small island, comprising only 224 square miles, connected to the southern tip of the Malay Peninsula by a stone and cement causeway (bridge) that carried railway tracks, a highway, and a pipeline across the Johore Strait.

Hundreds of junks and sampans (canvas-covered floating shops and homes) with their colorful, rag-patched sails crowded the harbor, along with large ships being loaded or unloaded. It was a bustling place even in 1935. We had been told that every race, color, and blood mixture dwelt together in Singapore, the place where East meets West. That wasn't hard to believe as we looked at that blend of people. About three out of four Singaporeans, we learned, were Chinese; and about fifteen out of every hundred people were Malays. Most of the other people in the city and country were Indians, Pakistanis, and Europeans.

We found ourselves preaching mostly to Chinese in a large, crowded church. While we were only there for two nights of meetings, we saw many souls saved and needs met.

We sailed next through the South China Sea to the crown colony of Hong Kong, a beautiful island-city whose name itself means "fragrant harbor." Our entrance into this large harbor preceded by only six years the bombing of this city by Japan (on the same day that Japan attacked Pearl Harbor—December 7, 1941).

It didn't take us long to understand the truth of the term "noisy China." About 98 percent of Hong Kong's people are Chinese. Men on the street selling their wares uttered loud, weird shrieks. People near the flat where we stayed played the radio or phonograph by their open windows—all in Chinese. In addition, there was the clatter of people walking, their shoes resounding on the cement pavement. There were people everywhere.

Then we were confronted with the strange smells of the Orient. It would take some getting used to for this boy from the wide open country down south. Incense sticks burned outside doors to the "god of the door" for protection. In the old city, there was the sweetish smell of burning opium seeping from the dark opium dens.

It seemed strange to see the women carrying heavy burdens while the men ambled ahead of them unconcernedly. Whenever we encountered this disregard for the status of women, something rose up inside me to protest.

The open, untidy shops wedged together along narrow streets intrigued me, but the food looked unappetizing. Ragged rickshaw runners bellowed for a clear path along the crowded streets. Yet there was another side to Hong

Kong in the beautiful downtown section where many of the English and Europeans lived. Here there were wide streets, modern architecture, and beautiful shops.

During the ten days we were in Hong Kong, we were busy with three services a day; but we had the joy of knowing that souls were being saved daily and others were being filled with the Holy Spirit and with power for living. And there were many healings.

The ancient religions of China have imposed dark superstitions upon the spiritually darkened people. The Chinese adhere to the ethics of Confucius, worship Buddhist deities, and subscribe to Taoist demonology. Strangely, their birth, marriage, and funeral functions often embrace the teachings of all three. This was grievous to us who realized that they are demon-inspired.

We saw heathen priests burning counterfeit paper money in the streets before a funeral procession, claiming that this was helping the dead pay his way through the spirit world. They place food before a corpse in a coffin for the dead to eat, and the rats devour it at night. Then the priests explain that the spirit of the dead took the food.

We learned of people who were afraid of certain trees because an evil spirit supposedly lived there. We observed them kneeling before idols, one of which held the sun in its hand, another the moon, and another a great drawn sword. Yet another possessed about fifty hands extending from all parts of the body. To these they give honor and glory. I thought about the many Old Testament passages that issue God's warnings against such practices.

Brother Carter wanted to continue through China to the borders of Tibet and Burma to visit the missionary graduates of his London Bible school. When it was about time to depart Hong Kong for Yunnanfu, I didn't know what to do. My funds until now had been adequate, thanks to the provision of God's people as we traveled along; but now I found myself with insufficient money to book passage on the boat to Hanoi and then the train for three days to the inner city. We had agreed to travel by faith and not discuss our personal finances. I committed the matter to prayer, not saying anything to Mr. Carter.

Right at this time a Chinese woman, who had come from the mainland to Hong Kong for an expensive operation, was miraculously healed by God at one of our meetings. When her healing was confirmed by the doctor, she immediately sought me out and placed into my hand the money she had brought with her for the medical expenses. Not only that, but she also brought three crates of food that she said we would need for the journey. Later we were to especially praise God for that food, for our survival in the hinterland would have been most difficult without it. Thanks to that lady, all my expenses for our entire ninety days to Tibet and back were met, with some to spare.

After a thrilling baptismal service for new converts, Howard Carter and I set sail once more. This time it was to be a stormy trip, across the Gulf of Tonkin in a small combination steamer. We docked in the muddy bay of Haiphong, French Indochina (Vietnam). The next morning we boarded a little mountain train for a three day journey into Yunnan Province, the most backward section of China. We carried our own food, as did the natives.

We had been told that the train would not be traveling at night, as the mountains were very high and it was a treacherous trip even in daylight. So we shared primitive "hotels" two nights with the resident rats and roaches on our way through the backside of the world. After crossing the border into mainland China at Laokay, the route became one of the most remarkable feats of engineering in the world. For the first time in my life, I became travel sick as the little French train swung us through what seemed like endless tunnels that pierced the towering peaks of China's mountains. The curves were actually so sharp that you could look out the window and see the rear coaches entering a tunnel you had just come out of. Soot and cinders were thrown back into the open windows. It was a hot and uncomfortable trip, to say the least.

On the afternoon of the third day, our train finally pulled into the ancient walled and guarded capital city of Yunnanfu, now called Kunming, in southwest China. From the station we rode by rickshaw through the rough, uneven, cobblestone streets crowded with strange sights and smells. As we passed through the huge gates of this old city, I looked up and saw guards standing overhead, guns in hand. There was much to see and observe. We gazed in wonder at the hieroglyphics and carvings in the magnificent architecture of the city.

Once again we noticed the people. Always my eyes were studying faces, and always they looked familiar— these precious souls I had seen in my vision. I noticed for the first time the hobbling Chinese women whose feet had been bound because of a fifteen-hundred-year-old custom that originated when a petty ruler sought as his bride the girl with the smallest feet. My heart ached for these people, so bound by superstition, who needed desperately to have more than their feet unloosed, but whose minds and hearts had been held captive for generations by false teachings.

In this land of few waterworks and fewer sewage systems, the stench was even worse than in Hong Kong.
Streets were jammed with people as well as animals. Don-
keys and mules were everywhere. Merchants pushed their
wares in wheelbarrows; others carried eggs, persimmons,
and other produce in huge, woven baskets suspended from
shoulder poles. Little girls played a game on the ground
that looked like our hopscotch, and often the baby of the
family would be securely strapped to their backs. What an
education I was getting! I didn't have much time to think
about the folks back home; but when I did, I said to myself
that no one would believe that rowdy Lester Sumrall was
seeing what he was seeing and doing what he was doing.

We stayed at a mission house where Howard Carter had
made arrangements. For two weeks we ministered in the
area of Yunnanfu to lepers, opium addicts, and those in
the mission stations up and down the railroad route. We
saw the heathen worshiping thousands of ugly gods. We
visited the slave girls' market located in the local jail.
There were twenty-four pitiful girls for sale. We went to a
German Christian orphanage where girls redeemed
(bought) by the missionaries were being taught from the
Bible and shown the love of God. They had clean clothes,
clean beds to sleep in, toothbrushes and personal items;
and they were learning needlework and other handcrafts.

In the evenings the missionary would blow his trumpet
in front of the large mission hall in the mission compound
where we were staying, and in five or ten minutes it would
be filled with Chinese. Interestingly, a wooden partition
built down the center of the mission hall separated the
men from the women while worshiping.

This was a very difficult mission field for these missionaries, and our hearts felt heavy for them. We knew we had to transfer this burden to the Lord, even as the missionaries assured us they did; and I learned the meaning of castings one's burden on the Lord and leaving it there (see Matt. 11:28) in those pre-World War II days in China.

Then it was time to move on once again. The next lap of our journey was to be an eighteen-day trip to other mission stations farther inland. The British and American consuls both advised against this journey, as the route was infested with robber bands and Communists who were looking for those they could capture for ransom.

We were reminded that American missionaries John and Betty Stam had fallen into the hands of Red forces that captured the city of Tsingteh on December 6, 1934, and that the ransom demand for their release had been set at twenty thousand dollars. It had been widely circulated that an army of two thousand Communists had increased to six thousand as it swooped down on the district, leaving many dead behind and carrying others away as captives. Terror reigned supreme, all who could had fled, and there was much looting. The Stams had been taken captive and forced on a treacherous, twenty-mile journey. Shortly thereafter they were painfully bound with ropes, their hands behind them. Then they were stripped of their outer garments and forced to walk through the streets of Miaosheo. Like their Master, they were led up a little hill outside the town. And there, in a clump of pine trees, they were forced to kneel. There was a quick command, the flash of a sword, and John and Betty Stam were ushered into the presence of their Lord. Just prior to this, Betty Stam had hidden their infant daughter, and she was rescued thirty hours later.

We heard all of this, and we knew these raving Red marauders were merciless. We had also been advised that this was the "wet season" and it was better not to travel unless it was very necessary. Not only roads, but entire villages had been known to be washed away by torrential rains. So we prayed and sought the Lord's leading. In the end, Carter felt it was God's will that we should go on, and I was of the same mind.

A Christian brother fitted us out with the kind of clothes we needed. He supplied us with zipperless knee-length trousers, which seemed baggy enough for me to wrap around myself three times. These were tied with a rope around our waist and tucked into knee-high boots. Over this we wore loose shirts and coats with buttons made out of knots of the same cloth. These were the traditional clothes for hinterland China. Along with these outfits, we were given oilskin capes.

We hired a cook and an interpreter and rented seventeen pack animals, including horses for us to ride on. The mules carried huge packs on each of their sides and wore V-shaped wooden saddles with our cots and bedding piled on top of that. Sometimes we sat astride the bedding, high above the wild country trail that was often only six feet wide.

Finally, it was time to bid adieu to the last ramparts of civilization for what would turn out to be nine very long weeks. The British consulate sent a guard of soldiers along with us for protection. Our destination? The borders of Tibet and Burma.

10

China before
Its Doors Were Closed

As our caravan headed west toward the Kikiang Mountains on the Tibet and Burma borders, we stopped at every little muddy village and in most of these remote outposts found missionaries from different countries. They represented Sweden, Holland, Germany, Australia, England, other parts of Scandinavia, and America; but there were no barriers of denominationalism or nationalism. The love of Christ bound us together as brothers in the Lord.

Several times we were thrown from our mules and horses, but no one was injured as we followed the narrow, slippery, rocky paths. As we journeyed through deep ravines and over narrow ledges at dazzling heights into the "Switzerland of China," we experienced the protective hand of God in our midst.

We saw many unusual sights, but I never became numb to the horror in my heart when I observed these Chinese people bowing and praying before idols. Several times we saw cornfields with burning incense sticks and lovely women bowing and praying in front of them for a good harvest. How much they needed to know about the Lord of the harvest!

Toward evening of a typical day, we would enter through the gate of the walled village, go past the tower of the guard and the white pagoda (which they believed protected them from the devils that would destroy their homes and bring plagues upon them), and dismount from our animals. As we led our animals through the village, we would have to push aside the pigs, dogs, and other animals and cry "Yield the way" to the people along the narrow, crowded streets. When we weren't staying in missionary compounds (because many of the villages didn't have missionaries), we stayed at "horse inns." These were frame buildings that housed the horses and mules on the ground floor and the guests above in the lofts.

These loft rooms were generally quite similar from village to village. Usually there was a home shrine with various idols differing in size and number according to the wealth of the family who owned the inn. Some grain, grass, or food might be on the primitive altar; and there were always some half-burned sticks of incense and vases of dead flowers, with dust and cobwebs everywhere. Sometimes in one corner of these rooms we would find a roughly made long box. We learned that this was the coffin waiting for the next person who died. Usually it was meant for the grandmother or grandfather.

A look into the next room might reveal one to eight men lying on a large, wooden bed smoking opium through water pipes.

When the slave girls called "Come to food," we would gather around a little table and receive a bowl of rice and a set of chopsticks. Soon our eyes would begin to smart because there were no chimneys to allow the smoke to escape. A sudden rifle report announced it was time to retire and begin the battle of the bedbugs.

All too soon the cock would be crowing, and we would hear the innkeeper and horsemen bustling about downstairs. It was time to arise, fold up the bedding and the cot, and get ready for breakfast before the day's long ride began. The farther we went, the more convinced I became that only a mountain mule such as I was riding could have climbed those mountains. The path at times was only as wide as the mule's feet, with a drop of a hundred feet or more to one side. I found myself reminding the Lord to keep His guardian angels alongside us!

But my heart always ached for the people—people crowded together with disease everywhere; deformed and burdened people; people crushed by sorrow and scarred by sin; people living in darkness and dying in darkness. And there were so many of them!

Sometimes we stopped to eat lunch in a stable yard among the pigs, chickens, and dogs and the Chinese men, women, and ragged little children. They all came, hoping for a morsel from the "rich man's table."

One night we slept in a barn with what seemed to be a million opium seed poppies that we had to push aside to set up our cots. This was the seed for the next year's sowing. We saw children as young as five years old, as well as ancient, shriveled men and women, smoking the dreadful poppy juice, which numbs the faculties and saps the vitality from their systems.

Another night we spent in a Buddhist lamasery with the immense figure of a tranquil Buddha overlooking our beds.

Eventually we gained the top of the Kikiang Mountains and looked upon the towering peaks of beautiful, tropical Burma to the south. We gazed longingly into the forbidden land of Tibet, which had not opened her doors to Christian missionaries.

In some of the villages we visited along the way, where women were the beasts of burden and cheaper than animals, the people were so primitive that they had never seen a watch. They lived in adobe huts and ground grain by rubbing stones together. We told them about Jesus and the love of God, and it seemed to us that they responded. The hunger in the human heart to know the God of the universe is the same, we found, wherever we went.

In the mid-thirties all ideas of democracy and freedom among the Chinese were being challenged by the Communists. By 1935, Chiang Kai-shek, a name that was to become very familiar to the world in succeeding years, and his armies were fighting the Communist forces in remote corners of China. It was a time of great instability and suffering. We saw places where entire villages had been plundered and burned. We saw dried pools of blood, stark evidence that large groups had been massacred. We heard stories of brutality beyond description, and we were constantly warned that we should get out of China. Eventually, not surprisingly, we had an encounter with some brigands.

We had climbed the hills of south China and descended into valleys on muleback for nine long weeks when we turned a bend on the trail and came face to face with three men in ragged uniforms who accosted us with their rifles drawn. Their cruel, scowling faces were enough to put fear into the heart of any mortal man, but in *our* hearts we cried out to God for protection and knew we had it.

Keeping us at gunpoint and without uttering a word, they followed behind us. Our Chinese horsemen, who usually joked among themselves, were silent and pale as death. But we just kept moving on. Finally, one of the men spoke. "We want money."

Our interpreter gave them not only money, but food. Then suddenly, with a terrifying scream and a signal from one of the bandits, the ragged trio disappeared into the bush. There was no reason for them not to murder us, but we lived to tell about it. We considered it a miracle of God's divine protection.

While on the borders of Tibet, ministering to the Lisu tribesmen, I stared at a man, knowing I had seen him before. I questioned him through my interpreter. Then the Lord let me know again that once more I was seeing one of the people from my vision. This man's face was one of the faces I had seen *clearly* in that long, endless line of people on the Road of Life. He was a part of my destiny.

Soon, however, on this venture into remote China, I wondered if I would fulfill the rest of my destiny. I had contracted an oriental dysentery. In spite of our prayers, it appeared that I would bleed to death. I had bloody diarrhea, pain, and fever for forty-eight hours before we started out on the trail again early one morning. I had no appetite and could hardly mount the mule to take my place at the end of the caravan. By eight o'clock, I could go no farther. I turned my little mule to the side of the trail, tied him to a bush, and lay down under it feeling very sure I was going to die. The caravan went on without me, evidently thinking I had just stopped for a moment. But as soon as I lay down, I passed out.

It was high noon when I awoke. I'd slept four hours. I was passing no blood; the fever and the pain were gone. I stood up and found that my strength had returned. I recognized I had been miraculously healed by God's mighty power.

But now I realized I was very much alone. I untied the mule, got on him, and gave him a little stick where it would do the most good. He changed from low gear (about three miles an hour) to high (about five miles an hour), and down that Chinese-Tibetan path we went! That evening about dusk I caught up with the caravan. Later that night, sitting on the side of my cot in one of the mud-walled "horse inns," I wrote in my diary: "I lay down to die and God healed me." Closing the diary, I closed my eyes for some much-needed sleep. The next morning I continued on around the world with Howard Carter.

Pre-World War II China presented a picture of great unrest and distrust of foreign influences. The church came under severe persecution, and missionary work was dangerous. The church was often identified with Western culture and all the problems of colonialism. We spent almost a year traveling throughout mainland China, but it was apparent that permanent trouble was brewing in this part of the world. Not only was there great internal trouble—incredible violence and suffering among the people—but the Japanese were presenting an external threat to China's security. We did not know that soon all doors for evangelism in China would be closed, but we did sense an urgency in our mission.

Howard Carter and I returned from Yunnanfu on the treacherous, little French railroad, back through Hanoi to

Haiphong, where we took a ship through the Gulf of Haiphong back to Hong Kong. From there we headed north into China again to visit more missions. Often we felt the world could never be saved. There was too little effort, too late—not enough missionaries, and even those few were ill-equipped. They found the strange Chinese culture to be a great hindrance to their efforts to reach these people for Christ.

We went from town to town, from city to city, seeing everything from wealthy lords and landowners to diseased and starving beggars living on rubbish heaps. Everywhere we went there was this contrast. In places there was the unbelievable beauty of China, with its rich, green countryside, the pagodas, teahouses, rice paddies, slender bamboos dipping into quiet pools, and lakes bridged by long, gracefully arched, covered walkways.

There was also the poverty, with its thousands of shacks made of bamboo, cardboard, scrap lumber, and tar paper, and the poverty-stricken peasants laboring under heavy burdens, using primitive methods for planting and harvesting their meager crops. We looked at the murky, polluted water that provided transportation and crop irrigation and was also used for all their daily needs—drinking, washing produce, cooking, bathing, and washing clothes. I could not help but think of John 4:13–14, where Jesus spoke of Himself as the water of life. I thought also of John 10:10, which speaks of having life more abundantly. These people were so pathetically poor, but their greatest tragedy lay in their spiritual poverty.

Mainland China itself is like fifty different countries within one border. Canton is a sprawling, cosmopolitan city with rushing automobiles, large business houses, and crowded streets. From there we caught the ferry, a boat with a large eye painted on the front to help direct it through the thousands of junks and sampans maneuvering through the river, to connect with the Fatshan train. We arrived in Fatshan at night and made our way down the main street, walking past the brightly lit shops decorated with Chinese writing. Families were having their evening meal in the doorways. And always there was the clatter of wooden clogs. Noisy China!

We stayed for a week of meetings, then continued back through Canton and on to Shanghai, a city of massive, modern buildings and an imposing waterfront. We ministered in a church that would hold fifty, while outside were six million Chinese tormented by devils and bound by evil. But the kingdom of darkness was no match for God's power. We saw many souls saved and delivered from Satan's grip.

In Shanghai a Nationalist youth, pointing at a Ford, said to me, "See our cars?"

"Yeah," I said, "they're made in America."

"No!" he countered. "I was going to ask you if you had any there."

"Yeah," I responded, "that's where these come from."

"No! Made here!" he insisted. "Made in China."

"Is Ford a Chinese word?" I asked him.

"Yeah! Ford Chinese word. Nothing like that made in capitalist country like America." He had seen a Chinese assembly line and was told it was a factory. The brainwashing of the Chinese was effectively being carried on.

Before flying up to Tientsin, we met several far-interior missionaries from Kansu who had been evacuated because of the Red menace. They spoke guardedly of uprisings and rebellions, the fear and insecurity of the people, the chaos and suffering, and the immense spiritual need.

The fourteen-passenger monoplane took us 670 miles into north China to Tientsin for another week of meetings, strictly among the Chinese, where we were impressed with how difficult it was to hold their attention. Right in the middle of an intense call to sinners to repent, or just before the climax of an interesting story, one of them would get up and leave and a dozen would follow. It was so disruptive that Carter and I resorted to different maneuvers to keep their attention. At times we would ring a little bell, clap our hands together, or speak in an unusual tone of voice. That may sound strange to you, but it was the thing to do in China. I was reminded of the apostle Paul's words, "That I might by all means save some" (1 Cor. 9:22).

Typical of the questions we were asked were these: "How many creations were there?" "Where did Cain get his wife?" "Why did God let man sin in the Garden of Eden?" One man asked a lot of questions and called himself a quarter-Christian. When he left the meeting, after experiencing the presence of God and the power of the Holy Spirit, he called himself a whole-Christian. For him, like the other Chinese who decided for Christ, it meant persecution from friends and family. In time, under the purge of Christians in China, it may have meant death. For those who escaped, it must surely have meant going underground with their faith, running for their lives at times, and not knowing from one day to the next what tomorrow held.

But we saw doctors, lawyers, businessmen, newspaper reporters, students, and men and women from all other walks of life kneel before the one true God and confess their sins and need of Christ. All during the war years and those long years when the doors to China were closed and so little information came out, I often found myself wondering about these precious brothers and sisters in Christ. I prayed much for them.

We rode the train eighty miles northwest to the terminal at Peking, the great imperial city of north China. There we engaged a rickshaw that took us through the massive city gates into the ancient capital city, with its flaming red, green, and gold-decorated, traditional architecture. To say I was awed at what I was seeing would be a considerable understatement—I was overwhelmed, and at times speechless, as I gazed about me.

One incident stands out in particular these many years later. As we were riding along in our rickshaw, drawn by a Chinese coolie, one of the other missionaries instructed his rickshaw runner to pull over close to ours and, pointing ahead, said, "We are approaching the British Legation. Take special notice of the wall to your right." As our runner slackened his pace, we saw a white wall upon which were inscribed in large, black letters three never-to-be-forgotten words: LEST WE FORGET. Upon closer observation, we could see perforations caused by many bullets. That made us even more curious to learn the history of the wall.

It was behind this wall, the missionary informed us, that a number of missionaries had taken refuge during the horrible Boxer Rebellion in 1900, when the dowager empress seized the civil government and demanded the death of all foreigners in China (many of these people were missionaries and their families). With murderous hearts, the

Boxers hunted down the "white faces" and slew them without mercy. One hundred eighty-nine Protestant missionaries and their children were killed before an armistice could be reached. One day the Boxers found some missionaries behind this Peking wall and fired upon them. When it seemed the wall would collapse and they must surely perish, some British marines, who had marched from Tientsin, arrived and valiantly drove the Chinese back, rescuing the missionaries. Many years ago I met marines who had fought the bloody battles of the Boxer Rebellion, and they confirmed the furiousness of the struggle.

We visited the Forbidden City, the imperial family's mile-square official residence that is now a public museum. It is surrounded by high walls and a moat, and on display are gorgeous throne rooms and priceless gifts of gold, silver, jade, ivory, and precious stones given by renowned people from all over the world years before. We saw very old paintings, elaborate royal household furnishings, thousands of heathen deities, and golden ceilings beaten and shaped into dragon heads. It all portrayed a vain and faded glory, which made us realize again that the glory of this world fades and passes away.

From Peking we traveled north by train to Kalgan on the Mongolian border for ten days of special meetings. We were privileged to stand on the Great Wall of China, built as a fearful, frantic effort to ward off devastating attacks from Mongolian invaders. As we stood there, I couldn't help but think of the more than 300,000 men who died while building this wall—human lives sacrificed in vain, for the wall failed to keep out the invaders. But it also reminded me of the walls of prejudice, hate, misunderstanding, and gross ignorance behind which these beautiful Chinese people still remained in bondage, walled in by the tyranny of communism and belief in superstition, magic, false gods, idols, and the teachings of Buddhism, Confucianism, and Taoism.

We arrived in Kalgan on a very windy day in the midst of a dust storm that burned our faces and chapped our lips. Here we had our first adventure on the backs of three large dromedaries (camels). We visited a mosque and saw the people prostrating to their deities.

We visited a Confucian temple on a hillside just outside the city walls. It was very old and renowned for its architectural beauty. There were fierce gods standing with swords drawn, with a serpent in hand, or with a number of dragon heads protruding from their bodies, ready to devour all who disobeyed or did not offer incense to appease their wrath. Nowhere could we find a god named the God of Love who would comfort and bless the people. I thought of Paul the apostle standing in the midst of Mars Hill, crying out:

> Ye men of Athens, I perceive that in all things ye are too superstitious. For as I passed by, and beheld your devotions, I found an altar with this inscription, TO THE UNKNOWN GOD. Whom therefore ye ignorantly worship, him declare I unto you. God that made the world and all things therein, seeing that he is Lord of heaven and earth, dwelleth not in temples made with hands. . . . For in him we live, and move, and have our being (Acts 17:22–24,28).

But we found that a beautiful spirit of fellowship prevailed among the Christians in Kalgan—love and cooperation had torn down denominational walls. Other missionaries came to worship with us, and it was good to know there was such a strong, united body of believers in that corner of the world.

For our final mission in China, we returned to Peking, where we held three services daily, dividing our time between American, British, and Swedish missions. The receptiveness of the people's hearts was a great encouragement—these were golden opportunities to preach the gospel. Little did we know how much this would mean to these Chinese in the long years ahead.

More and more of the far-inland missionaries were having to evacuate their stations as the communists took over the territory. The Japanese army had already captured much of north China, and banks were being looted. We rode in trains loaded with China's silver and gold that was headed for Japan. We did not realize we were witnessing the start of a second world war. The doors for evangelism in China were closing. Satan was going to make an all-out effort to stamp out Christianity.

It may never be known just how many Chinese brothers and sisters in the Lord were executed for their faith. Tens of thousands of Christians were tortured and imprisoned. Churches and mission stations were confiscated and turned into government entertainment centers, factories, and warehouses. Seminaries were closed. Religious literature was destroyed. All missionaries were forced to leave China. The Christians in China truly passed through "the valley of the shadow of death." How grateful we were that it had been our joy and privilege to be there sharing the good news of the gospel and the Lord's promise that He is with us always.

11

The Land of the Morning Calm and the Land of the Rising Sun

Back in Tientsin we boarded the train heading toward Korea, but we first crossed the border of north China into Manchuria, a large territory south of Siberia, north of China, with Korea on the east and Mongolia on the west. It was in November 1935 that we first saw a lovely, snow-covered landscape (the first snow we had seen since leaving our home countries). By 4:30 in the afternoon, when we arrived in Mukden, it was bitterly cold and the streets were icy. In Mukden we learned that many local Christians had been imprisoned as anti-Japanese instigators. (Manchuria was Japan's puppet state.) This made people afraid to venture out to church services.

North of Mukden was Harbin, Manchuria's great, cosmopolitan city. It was even colder when we arrived there, and the river was frozen to such a depth that we saw large trucks passing over the ice. We weren't prepared for what else we saw there—frozen bodies lying in the street. Beggars had stolen their clothing; others kicked them to one side to let the traffic pass. We saw beggar women, some with children in their arms, shaking with cold and dying of hunger, screaming for help, begging passers-by for a few pennies to buy opium. My heart broke for these souls for whom Christ died.

We then boarded the train once more and headed for Korea, the Land of the Morning Calm, also called the Hermit Kingdom. Korea, the crossroads of the Orient, is situated between Japan and China and dates back across four thousand years of bloody history.

Korea's first Christian missionary was almost an instant martyr. Within a few moments of landing on the shore with his arms full of tracts and Gospels of John, he was stoned by the men of the city.

In Seoul, where we learned to return bows with the natives three or four times, we also learned to take our shoes off at the door and put on the soft slippers that were provided. Unlike the Chinese, the Koreans sit quietly on their little, straw mats and listen attentively. In the evening we had a service scheduled at an out-station. First we had to take the tram to the downtown district, then an electric train to the suburbs, next a paddle boat (loaded with oxen, carts, and people) across the river; and then we walked for about fifteen minutes through deep sandbeds and finally arrived at the village. The meeting was held in a school building, with paper lanterns and one small, oil lamp casting eerie shadows on the walls. But the crowd was large and responsive to the preaching of the Word.

We took a boat to the main island of Japan and found that traveling there was not as primitive as in China and Korea. The scenery was gorgeous—beautiful orchards of ripe, luscious fruit, with snow-capped Mount Fuji in the background. The train stations were ultramodern for 1936.

On January 1, everybody has a holiday in the Orient, since that is everyone's birthday. There are new clothes and elaborate feasts to celebrate the day. The Japanese love beauty; they enjoy their gardens and often take tours to see flowers and trees. They are also a very courteous people, we discovered, even though Americans were not very popular in Japan at the time we were there. The nation was siding with Hitler and getting ready to make a gigantic push into Asia.

We began our itinerary with twenty-one meetings in two weeks. Tokyo, the capital city, was our starting place. Meetings were held at the Takinogawa Church Bible School. Mr. Carter lectured to the Bible school students during the day, and I preached in the evening services. For the most part the missionaries and those Japanese who already were Christians attended the meetings. We saw some conversions; others were filled with the Holy Spirit.

From Tokyo we headed south to Harmantan for meetings and then to Nagoya (where the children screamed with laughter at my English articulation). Then on to the fascinating city of Kyoto, the "Classic City," for a thousand years the capital and famous for its bygone days of splendor. Everywhere we went the Christians were open-hearted and kind, but we continued to feel that our presence in the country at that time was, at best, subject to suspicion.

The most astounding thing we discovered in Japan was the revival of the ancient religions of Buddhism and Shintoism, with masses of believers pursuing them. They had emulated Christianity by erecting schools, constructing large orphanages, opening seminaries, and sending forth militaristic disciples. They had sought and obtained what we could only regard as a devilish power resembling spiritism, which they actually called the "Holy Spirit." It was the devil's counterfeit of the pentecostal blessing, but they claimed to have supernatural power to relieve pain and sickness.

I was horrified to see two Americans who had joined the Buddhist priesthood, shaved their heads, and put on long, flowing robes, and who now were begging rice from shop to shop as is the custom of the priests.

My personal opinion of Japan, after visiting her largest cities as well as her small towns, was that the so-called Christian nations had given Japan a hunger and thirst for Western civilization, had brought her from medieval obscurity into the global limelight, but had miserably failed in quenching that deep inner hunger and thirst that all men have to know the true God. I did not feel Christianity was flourishing in Japan. I found Japan, with all her enlightenment and progress, to be one of the most difficult fields for soul-winning. We continued on our itinerary, and, although the results were not spectacular, we were encouraged to see scores of Japanese born into the Kingdom of God.

We returned by boat and train to Seoul, Korea, where the temperature had dropped to six degrees below zero. We were there to encourage our new converts to stand fast and rejoice with those who had been healed on our previous visit. The Koreans were preparing for the Chinese New Year, a celebration that begins on January 24 (calculated by the lunar calendar) and continues for fifteen days.

During this time the people neither work nor worry, but feast and worship their gods.

We learned that at this season they tear down all their paper gods and put up new ones. The "god of the kitchen" gets a small piece of paper pasted over his mouth before he is torn down, so that he won't be able to tell any bad tales about what he has seen or heard during his reign of a year. The "god of the door" rides on a mystical, ferocious beast and holds a great, broad sword in his hand. He has now finished his mission of protection and is torn down to be replaced by a new one, painted in blazing colors.

Thousands of little home and roadside shrines are decorated with bright red paper with large, black picture-painting letters on them. As we passed along the road, we saw incense sticks burning and little piles of grain or dishes of food being offered up to the gods. The Chinese were eager to start the new year right with favor from their gods. But not all the Korean Chinese were taken up with the heathen festival and the worshiping of idols. It was a brief stay, but we were able to minister to the saints and see their faith increase, and there were some sinners who were made to see that the power of Jesus Christ is real. On the Chinese New Year we left Korea to continue north, to Port Arthur, Manchuria, for special meetings.

From Port Arthur we once again journeyed north to Mukden, where we ministered for several days in a local church. We also watched a strange burial custom. A heathen man who lived across from the church died. His family sent for musicians, who came and sat in the gateway, playing weird, unearthly music on Chinese instruments while another person sang to the dead man. In the afternoon a great paper horse of diverse colors, pulling a cart, was delivered to the man's door so that his spirit would not have to walk on his journeys through the spirit world.

Every night for several days, six or seven priests performed ceremonial rites over the dead body. They had candles lit on a table with a number of different kinds of food placed before them. At one end of the coffin were five dishes of food for the dead man, which the priests ate themselves while talking to him. Eventually, they carried the corpse out to the burial ground with a procession. Twenty-five men carried the coffin on large, beautifully and richly decorated poles. As they went, they scattered false money by the hundreds and thousands of dollars to pay the dead man's way through the spirit world.

We saw this type of thing in several countries. Always I found it disheartening, and it made me very sad. My education continued in these and other ways as I observed the heathen customs and realized how much these people needed the truth of the gospel.

From Mukden we traveled north again to Harbin, with its communities of Russians, Germans, Poles, Japanese, and Chinese, besides a few hundred English-speaking people. We ministered at the Russian Eastern European Mission Station to a congregation of White Russians who had escaped the communists. As I looked into the faces of these emigrants who had escaped from the Bolshevik reign in Russia, I saw expressions of grief and hardness of countenance resulting from the privation and persecution they had endured. These were displaced, embittered individuals; but as we poured out our hearts to them, assuring them that Jesus loved them and that He understood, we saw their hearts become tender. They began to weep their way to the foot of the cross as they learned about how Jesus had suffered and died for them.

This ended more than a year of ministry and travel throughout the Orient. In my heart I knew that, the Lord willing, in the years ahead I would return whenever possible to minister to these hungry souls who needed the Bread of Life.

12

The Land
of Spies and Suspicion

"What is your occupation?"

"Minister, sir."

"Minister of what?"

"Minister of religion."

"Ah, yes. Well, that's a different matter."

It was in the Russian Consulate in Harbin, Manchuria, that this crisply punctuated conversation took place. Howard Carter and I were seeking a transit visa to cross into Siberia and the USSR and on into Poland. Our passports were in order, but the consul didn't quite understand the word "minister."

When we explained that we were involved in missionary work, he stated, "Well, we will have to wire Moscow to get special permission for you to pass through the Soviet Union. The reply may take as long as two or three weeks, and it will cost you eighteen dollars."

This was more than a little exasperating. It called forth our holy anger! "What?" I said. I was outraged. "Do you mean that just because we're ministers of the gospel, we can't travel as ordinary tourists?"

"Yes, you will have to have a special permit from Moscow. This is our law," he answered.

"But, why? Are we criminals evading justice or something?"

"No," he said, "only that you are preachers."

We explained that we had special engagements in the country and that time was of the essence. We couldn't afford to lose any days. "Besides that," I added, "we have already bought our tickets to Poland."

He assured us he would do the best he could and would add the word *urgent*. "Maybe the answer will come in four or five days," he stated weakly.

We thanked him for his help and assured him that we appreciated his kindness. But by the day of our scheduled departure, there was no response from Moscow. We had to stay put, and now our anger was joined by growing frustration. The visas arrived the following day, but as the trans-Siberian trains ran only every four days, we had to send a telegram to Poland and postpone the meetings.

Finally, on February 17, 1936, we were allowed to board the Chinese Eastern Railroad Northwest train to Manchouli, the Siberian frontier station. There we transferred to the single-track Trans-Siberian Railway for the 5,800 mile, nine-day ride on the loneliest railroad route in the world. Our transfers were accepted, however, only after a scrutinizing customs examination to be certain we had no religious or political tracts to distribute. As soon as we crossed the border into Siberia, our belongings were again searched and our passports and tickets taken into custody, leaving us with no identification. From that time on, we were under surveillance day and night by special guards.

What we saw through the frosty windows of that train can never be erased from my memory. The first thing that attracted my attention was a large, crimson-colored flag hoisted above the station in the wilds of Siberia where we stopped the following morning. It gently moved in the breeze, but I knew its gentle movement was not characteristic of what that flag signified. Then I noticed three large portraits hanging where they couldn't be missed in the station—and the hard expressions on the faces of Stalin, in the center, and Lenin and Marx, on the sides.

In the Siberian wilderness the temperature dips at times to fifty below zero. Not only was it bitter cold outside, but we were also to sense the coldness of the hearts of the officials with whom we had to brush shoulders from time to time.

Around the station were a number of poorly clad people with expressions of privation and depression written across their faces. About the village were a number of small log cabins. We passed a crew of log-men working by the railway, and we could see their faces distinctly—faces lined with fatigue, showing the stress to which they were subjected. To one side stood a well-dressed soldier with his rifle, watching the crew work. No doubt it was a camp of exiled men, suffering terrible hardship. These Siberian prison camps, we had been told, were literally prisons for the living dead—hollow-eyed, ragged creatures, loading and unloading the trains. Some of them were guarded by armed men with vicious dogs.

We observed how hard communism was on the women. Ninety percent of the snow diggers and railway-yard workers were poorly clad, haggard-looking women. At every station we saw the red flag, the portraits of their pitiless oppressors, and the same pathetic-looking people. We saw hundreds of little dugouts and caves, which we assumed were the "homes" for these depressed and oppressed men and women. I saw more snow than I had ever seen before in my young life. It is no wonder that Siberia is referred to as a land of frozen wastes. And it is no wonder that the czars and dictators of Russia have sent millions of their enemies and criminals to these cold and isolated parts of this dreary country—there is no way they could escape and live to tell about it. I couldn't help but wonder how many of these exiled people were Christian brothers and sisters who had been banished to live out their days here because of their faith.

Aboard the train was an "Intourist" interpreter for the aid of the English-speaking passengers. We asked him about general conditions in Russia. Some of his answers sounded truthful, but many of them didn't. We were told that the economic situation was better than it had ever been before; that the collective farmers and the peasant population had enough food and clothing; that manufacturing was growing by leaps and bounds; and that since they had abolished the stock exchange at that time, the gold ruble was stabilized and profiteering had been eliminated, thereby giving more money to the common people.

Russia, at the time, was preparing for the greatest war in history; but we, of course, did not know this. We asked about religious conditions and were told, "No one is forbidden to pray or worship God." The interpreter could not (or would not) explain why we had been delayed and treated as we had at the Russian Foreign Affairs office.

Many years have passed since our trip through those Siberian wastelands, and in the interim, information has seeped out into the Western world about what it is like to be arrested and sent away. Aleksandr Solzhenitsyn was instrumental in opening many eyes to the brutality and horrors of concentration camp living. He spoke of arrest as "a breaking point in your life, a bolt of lightning which has scored a direct hit on you . . . an unassimilable spiritual earthquake not every person can cope with, as a result of which people often slip into insanity."

In Moscow, the Mecca of socialism, the Jerusalem of communism, we had about a five-hour wait; so we asked the tourist official about a sight-seeing tour. He told us that a trip to the places they would permit us to visit would take about an hour by taxi and cost thirty-five rubles. We were driven past the large hotels and business houses of the city, owned and operated by the government (there not being a privately owned place of business in Russia). We were shown the great opera, cinema, and theater houses where the Soviets gather and attempt to enjoy their plays and films depicting Russian Communist glory.

Next our guide showed us the large apartment houses for government employees. Then we came to the Soviet Square and the statue of liberty where the guide said the Great Revolution of 1917 started. We were then taken to famous Red Square, where we saw Lenin's red marble mausoleum and his body embalmed in a glass casket. This is the place where blood ran down the streets in the horrible revolution when the czar was driven from power. Red Square is the scene of a huge May Day parade every year in honor of working people.

We saw the ancient and artistic edifice of old Saint Basil's Church, which at one time was a place of worship but is now used as a museum. The architecture of Old Russia is represented by many-colored, onion-shaped domes like those of Saint Basil's Church. We asked about these old churches and were told that they now are used as cabarets, clubs, museums, or anything that has to do with profit or pleasure for the Communist party.

We saw the grand Kremlin Palace, the meeting place of the Supreme Soviet of the USSR, Russia's parliament. The structure of the Soviet government, like that of its Communist party, resembles a pyramid. But it has long been known that the people who run the Communist party run Russia.

At the time we passed through Russia, during the mid-thirties, the people were living under extreme terror; and the secret police were arresting millions of Russians suspected of having anti-Communist views or participating in anti-government activities. These victims were either shot or sent to the prison camps. Many of these people had openly opposed Stalin's policies during the mid-1930s. In order to crush this opposition, Stalin began a program called the Great Purge. It was that, indeed, as great terror spread across the land. Millions of people were arrested by the secret police. Even family members spied on each other. Fear and suspicion spread throughout the nation. We were there right at this time.

We noticed a marked difference between the dress of the soldiers and the government officials and that of the ordinary people on the street. The government employees were well-dressed; the common people had on the old

Russian felt boots to their knees and wore shabby, worn-looking clothes. But on their faces they wore what was even more heartbreaking—forlorn looks of misery.

The Communists were doing everything possible to discourage religious practices through their propaganda and educational efforts. The Russian Orthodox church was the official Russian church before the Communists rose to power. But the Communists destroyed or confiscated most of the churches. Many church leaders were killed; others were imprisoned. In spite of present-day propaganda coming out of the Soviet Union, which would indicate that churches today have reopened and people are allowed to worship freely, religious life in Russia is not at all what you and I are accustomed to.

We acquired a Moscow newspaper printed in English. Not surprisingly, it was full of Communist activities and propaganda. One article struck us forcibly, as we felt it depicted the sentiment of those who had sold out to the Communist party: "We will live for communism and we will die for communism." My heart swelled within me in a sort of holy zeal—how much more should we, as the followers of the Lord Jesus Christ, live for Him and, by His all-sufficient grace and mercy, die for Him if need be?

What a relief it was to reboard our train and continue west! What a relief to leave this land of spies and suspicion! What a pleasure to pass over the Russian border into a God-fearing country! As we neared the border, our tickets and passports were returned. At one o'clock in the afternoon we arrived in Stolbce, the Polish border city. From there Carter and I caught the next train to the city of Lodz, by way of Warsaw, arriving at two the next morning, very tired. Having heard the clacking and shrieking of locomotive wheels for more than nine days, we were now relieved to break the journey. It was good to be met by Christians and to know that we would be enjoying the warm fellowship of our beloved Polish Christian brethren.

13

Into the Heart of
the European Continent

The Poland of the mid-1930s was far different from the Poland that was to emerge after the enormous destruction and suffering that took place during World War II. Unfortunately for these brave people, Poland lay in the path of Hitler's expansionist objectives; and these dear people were to take the brunt of attacks from both Russian and German troops.

Again, we had no way of knowing it, but only three years following our visit, on September 1, 1939, Hitler's troops were to swoop into Poland from the west. And on September 17 the Russians, claiming they had to "protect" their borders, invaded the country from the east. The Poles fought valiantly, but they were no match for their enemies. This tug of war between Germany and Russia found Poland partitioned and coming under Russian control. But all that was after our time. Later, as we were to watch these wartime events unfolding and receive reports through the radio and in the newspapers, our hearts were torn as we thought of the people who had befriended us, whom we had come to love and appreciate in the five-and-a-half weeks we were there.

We found Poland to be a land of plains and gently rolling hills, a land with a long history and a rich cultural heritage. There was a strong sense of national loyalty and patriotism. We found eager, hungering souls in Poland. On our first Sunday there, we saw the people dressed in their best clothes going to places of worship. No stores were open; no business was being transacted. What a contrast this was to the Orient.

It was a joy to travel in Poland from one quaint village to the next. We were welcomed by overflowing crowds in the mission halls and churches. In 1936, Poland already had almost a thousand years of Christianity in its history; and Catholicism was very strong in that country. But we found people who were eager to hear our message—people who dearly loved the Lord and would walk for days to hear the Word of God preached. Some had never seen a foreign minister. Many came from miles away in springless wagons. Others walked in snow fifty miles or more with willow bark shoes tied to their feet. Whole villages would declare a holiday and come to the services. Many had no assurance that when they got there they would have bed or board, but sleeping on the floor or on straw was a small inconvenience for the privilege of hearing the gospel preached in power.

In one small town, Vilno, on the way to Warsaw, we were able to talk with the Jews in a Jewish mission about the love and power of Jesus Christ, of whom their forefathers shouted, "Let Him be crucified!"

In one of our services, a woman on the front row of the packed auditorium repeatedly said "Hallelujah" in a shrill, eerie voice. To myself I thought, "That doesn't sound right," but the local people didn't seem to notice or mind. Although she appeared to be religious, her interruptions were interfering with the message. I sensed that it was an evil spirit prompting the woman's strange behavior. I leaned across the pulpit, looked down at her, and called out, "Would you please shut up!" My interpreter looked at me as if I were crazy. But I repeated it and he said it in Polish. At that point she started barking like a dog. I shouted, "Now, I command you to come out of her!"

The woman jumped up, and a transformation took place. Her face became normal; her eyes lost their glassy look. She looked around at the people as though she were seeing them for the first time. At that, the Spirit of God came over the audience, and they began to cheer. She was set free! It was in this manner in several cities that I came to understand the exorcism of evil and that the power of the Holy Spirit delivers the same in the Orient, on the continent of Europe, or anywhere on the face of the globe when Jesus Christ is challenged.

We saw souls catch a spark from the heavenly altar in those weeks of Polish ministry. Those were some of the hardest and most tiring weeks of our tour, but they were also times of continual blessing. We thanked God often in later years that we had been there, and we prayed earnestly for those oppressed people.

From Poland we entered prewar Germany, a land of swastikas and rampant Semitic hatred. Hitler and his Nazi followers were already beginning to build Germany into a mighty war machine. The city of Berlin had not yet been divided, of course, and we found that permission had been obtained for us to hold a series of revival campaigns. It was nearing Easter.

For six days we ministered in the oldest Full-Gospel church in Berlin. On Good Friday we were invited to a Baptist convention, for which a group of churches had taken a large school auditorium. Then on Saturday and Easter Sunday we met in another large church. Every place was packed to the limit, and the traditionally staid Germans responded with fervor to the messages. In one of our last meetings, we were warned that a Gestapo man was there; and his presence seemed to bind the liberty we usually felt in our meetings.

Leaving these services and going out in the streets of Berlin presented a contrast. There we saw men and boys giving each other the Nazi salute of raised open hand with curved thumb and greeting each other with "Heil Hitler!" It was unnerving. We did not have the liberty to preach for special services. Thus, there were difficulties, but the faith of those saints was strong, and our fellowship was sweet.

I witnessed the human comedy of international hypocrisy in Berlin. The city was preparing night and day for the great Olympic Games to be held there in 1936. Huge amphitheaters and stadiums were being built. The airport was being enlarged fourfold, while a huge military airport was under construction. Streets were being taken up and repaved. We saw public buildings, streets, parks, and homes festooned with five-link chains, representing the five continents—a fraternity of all colors, racial equality, and intercontinental unity in sportsmanship. Elaborate military highways were being built to crisscross the nation.

But there was mockery in all this—while playing at peace, they were secretly working at war.

After our ten-day visit, we bade a reluctant farewell to our German friends, feeling somehow that we would never fellowship with them again on these terms. It was a heavy sad feeling. We were saddened to learn shortly after this that most of the churches were closed and padlocked by Hitler in his madness. The mighty German war machine was closing in on its own people. Hitler's underlings were seizing control of the nation's courts, industries, newspapers, schools, churches, and police forces. Soon Hitler would spread death as no man had ever done before.

But now we were on our way, in what was to be the final leg of our tour, to the glorious Land of the Midnight Sun. Scandinavia was next on our itinerary. Mr. Carter and I had been invited to conduct special services in Oslo at the great Filadelfia Temple (Church of Brotherly Love), which was the largest in Norway. Thousands packed this tremendous church, with hundreds of people standing on the outside. The spiritual hunger in the hearts of these people was so real. We found this same hunger in Stockholm, Sweden, and in Copenhagen, Denmark. Perhaps it was a portent of what was to come—unknown to these people, but somehow sensed in their hearts.

We moved on to the great cities of Holland— Amsterdam and Rotterdam. Everywhere we preached the Lord confirmed His Word with signs following. Mr. Carter had been experiencing attacks of malaria, which is accompanied by fever and aches. In Sassenheim, Holland, when he suffered an acute attack, we canceled our engagements for Belgium, France, and Switzerland and flew directly to his home in London.

Our journal-keeping suffered on the last legs of this European trip (probably because of Carter's recurrent malarial flare-ups, which necessitated my taking over more of the meetings). But according to our records, we had averaged six hundred to a thousand miles a week through thirty countries and the islands of the sea. All totaled we traveled about sixty thousand miles, preaching in eighteen foreign languages with the help of sixty-five interpreters. It had been, from start to finish, a faith-walk. But I knew that my journey wasn't over; this would be a continuing walk for me. I now had more of a desire to reach the lost masses of the world than when I had begun.

14

Prelude to War

When we arrived in London, Howard Carter immediately went to bed with the ague—the fever and chills common to malarial symptoms. We stayed at the Hampstead Bible Institute. I traveled some doing crusades while Mr. Carter rested and regained his strength. Between meetings I was able to do some lecturing at the Bible school on evangelism, teaching the students from our many experiences.

Mr. Carter was chairman of the Assemblies of God Fellowship in the British Isles. It was time for their annual conference, which was to be held in Crosskeys, Wales. He was well enough to attend the conference and hold meetings the following week. Shortly thereafter, after much prayer asking God to undertake for him, Mr. Carter was healed; and we were able to continue on our missionary journey around the world together.

In Cardiff, Wales, I was privileged to share a ministry with the incomparable Smith Wigglesworth. Wigglesworth was noted for his miracle-studded ministry. He had the faith of an Elijah. I was twenty-three; he was eighty. In his home in Bradford, Midlands, where I visited him many times in ensuing years, he confessed to me that he danced before the Lord for ten minutes every morning, that he never allowed a newspaper in his house, and that he never asked himself how he felt. This man had a positive, dynamic faith. On my last visit to his home before returning to America, he said, "I am going to ask God to bless you with my spirit."

I knelt before him that memorable day. He placed his hands on my shoulders and prayed, "God, let the faith that is in my heart be poured into the heart of this young man. And Lord, let the works that I have seen You do be done in his life; let the blessing that You have given to me be his. Let the holy anointing that has rested upon my life now rest upon his life." From that time onward I sensed a new dimension of power in my preaching and ministry for the Lord.

After three months more on the European continent, Howard Carter and I crossed the Atlantic. On the seventh day, our boat steamed into the glorious St. Lawrence River channel and on to the great city of Montreal, Quebec, Canada. We were greeted in the harbor by an eighty-foot-tall electric cross with 250 high-powered bulbs. It was a never-to-be-forgotten sight. We traveled by train to Hamilton, Ontario, to preach at a Pentecostal general conference.

I was almost twenty-four, and I was much more mature—seasoned, I suppose you could call it—than the young man who had stood alone on deck as the ship left San Francisco some years before. I had been tutored by Howard Carter and blessed by Smith Wigglesworth.

But God was hard at work doing something from the inside. His power would surge through me with a force that made me unafraid of anything, anybody, or any situation.

One afternoon a friend took us over to see magnificent Niagara Falls. We looked at this majestic spectacle and heard its deafening roar, standing under its perpetual rainbow-colored spray; and our hearts magnified our omnipotent God. The power that I saw there seemed reflected in my own heart. I stood in awe at what God had done through Howard Carter and myself in our travels, and I realized that the same God who controlled the forces of nature controlled our destinies.

From there Carter and I separated for a brief while. I had appointments to minister in New York City, Washington, D.C., and Philadelphia. Then I was going to make my way south to see my parents, who had moved to Mobile, Alabama.

I was constantly filled with amazement that God should have chosen me to see and do the things I'd seen and done in so many different countries. Now I was ministering in places in the United States that I'd only read about before in history books or the paper. Sometimes I felt my eyes must have been bulging as I tried to take it all in. At other times I wished my neck were a swivel—there was so much to see, and I couldn't take it all in as I looked first here and then there. It was thrilling!

The reunion with my parents was joyful. I was always conscious that the prayers of my God-fearing mother followed me; now it was good to hold her in my arms. We spent many hours talking. There was so much to tell, and I knew she would want to discuss it all with the ladies from her prayer group.

While in Mobile I had a most unusual experience. A Christian woman made this request: "Lester, read some of the entries in your diary for me while you were in China."

So I opened it and began reading. At one place I read: "Today I expected to die. At 8 A.M. I dismounted from my mule, tied him to a tree, and lay on the ground. I awoke at noon. I lay down to die but God healed me."

The woman was sobbing.

"Don't cry," I said. "I didn't die!"

She held out her own diary. "Here, read," she said. I looked at the scrawled words and saw that at ten o'clock at night she had felt God was speaking to her, telling her I was dying. She had cried out, "Oh, no, Lord. Don't let him die." Then the diary revealed that for the next two hours she had continued in intercessory prayer for me. At midnight when she heard "He is healed," the burden lifted. She made the entry in her diary and fell asleep.

When it's ten o'clock in the morning in Tibet, it's ten o'clock at night in Mobile. When it's noon in Tibet, it's midnight in Mobile. In other words, her intercession on my behalf had been supernaturally guided, and such prayer power is one of the weapons with which we can defeat the devil and win the world to the Lord Jesus Christ.

After that needed respite at home and some of my mother's good cooking, I was once again ready to leave. I was scheduled to speak in St. Louis, Chicago, and South Bend, Indiana. In St. Louis a pastor asked me to accompany him on a visit to the home of one of his church members. We walked up the steps to the porch of the humble, little frame cottage. He knocked on the door, and the lady of the house let us in. She took us across the room to a rocking chair where a young man sat, staring into space. "This boy needs your help," the pastor said. One look at that boy and I knew I was once again being confronted with what I'd seen in Java, China, Japan, Poland, Germany, and England. I clamped my hands on both sides of that boy's head and commanded the demon to come out: "You unclean spirit, come out of him now!"

Then I said to the boy, "Speak, son, speak to your mother."

A shudder ran through the young man's body. He blinked and blinked again. Slowly, he turned his face toward his kneeling mother and held out his hand to her. "Oh, Mama," he said, "Mama, what happened?"

What had happened? The young man had attended a spiritist's meeting and during the seance had gone into a catatonic stupor from which he could not be roused. He hadn't spoken for more than three months; now he was speaking. When we left the house he was walking, talking, and praising God.

As we left I turned to my pastor friend and said, "I wouldn't have believed that this could happen in Christian America. The Orient, yes, and in other countries, yes, but certainly not here at home." This gift of discerning of spirits was operating through me freely, enabling me to recognize people who needed deliverance. It was not to be my last such encounter.

For the next six months I preached in churches across the country. Howard Carter flew down to Brazil for a special Bible conference, and now it was time for me to follow a few days later by ship.

While traveling from Joinville up to Santos, a two or three day journey up the coast on a freight boat carrying a heavy load of logs, a storm arose on our first night out to sea. I had never seen such a storm in my entire life. Our one-hundred-foot boat was like a peanut tossed on those mountainous waves. The waves broke over the old ship, and salt water penetrated every crack and crevice. Even our cabin on the top deck was filled to about twelve inches, and our belongings bobbed and floated back and forth across the room. It was all we could do to stand upright and maintain our balance by holding on to the bunk rails.

The captain made his way to our door, screaming, "We're sinking! Pray!"

At the same moment, my mother was praying for me in her church. She had seen a vision of my drowning at sea and was in travail. A Baptist preacher saw the light on in the church and came to the door. Once inside he saw a vision of Jesus walking down the aisle. He fell to his knees, and God baptized him with the Holy Spirit. He went to his own church and prayed all night in the grove behind it. Finally, at dawn, the Lord gave him assurance that all was well, and in his inner spirit he heard, "A boat had passed by and picked him up." And that is exactly how I was rescued.

The preacher returned to my mother's church, found her still praying, and said to her, "Your son is all right. God has spoken to my heart. Go home now and go to bed."

We spent several months in Brazil, at one time traveling by bus through the great Brazilian forest far inland from the coastal cities to visit an encampment of Lettish colonists from Latvia. They had come in the early 1920s to escape the scourge of communism, which was already sweeping through northern Europe at that time.

We learned their story. They had almost been annihilated by exposure to the tropical climate, by fevers and disease, alligators and other man-eating reptiles, coarse food, and unfriendly Indians; but they stuck it out. They prayed, trusted God, and earnestly, continually sought His help. They built a Christian community far from the hustle and bustle of the twentieth century. We had a precious time together.

We also traveled straight across the vast and desolate state of Mato Grosso (great forest). The mighty Amazon River and its tributaries flow through this region. Some of the area had never been explored. Big-game hunters are attracted to this part of the country to shoot jaguars, mountain lions, and crocodiles. I didn't have any desire to step out of the jumping, jerking train. The prairie dust mixed with the perspiration on our bodies, and we knew we were in the tropics.

But one thing we found to be incredible—even in that backside of the world, the conductor made us wear our coats on the train. We found this very strange; but in that part of the world, at that time, you wore a coat or risked getting fined. Worse, in the humid jungle you might even be put off the train! Even beggars are careful to wear coats in those countries. Occasionally I saw men or boys without pants, but never without a coat!

We met a missionary whose life's goal was to see a Bible placed in every Brazilian home. He told us the Indians believe there are two gods—a good one and an evil one. The good one, of course, would do them no harm: therefore, they only worshiped the evil one so they wouldn't incur his wrath. I shook my head on that—I'd heard lots of strange things in my travels, but this was one of the strangest. And when I heard that some of these people would even go so far as to sacrifice their children to placate the evil god's wrath, my heart was deeply burdened. I knew I would want to come back to this corner of God's earth to speak the truth.

We had hoped to go through Paraguay and on into Argentina, but an epidemic of yellow fever had broken out in the Paraguayan capital, and all international traffic was paralyzed indefinitely. After prayer, we decided to forgo the rest of our planned itinerary through South America and go on to Portugal.

I had seen enough of this part of the world—even though it was a whirlwind trip—to know that I wanted to return. I had observed the Indian and his religion, his superstitious beliefs, and how easily he fell prey to occultism and spiritism. How much they needed to hear about Jesus and His love!

Our thirteen-day voyage on the R.M.M.V. *Highland Chieftain* from the tropical southern waters to the European seaboard proved to be one of the most pleasant trips on our journey. Soon after we entered the estuary of the Tagus River, the beautiful city of Lisbon came into view, as well as two or three formidible-looking submarines, keeping an alert eye on incoming vessels. We were met by a Swedish missionary who conducted us to a former Roman Catholic church that was now their mission. There we were outfitted with heavy clothes, since the winter is severe in Portugal.

For fifteen days we held special meetings in northern

and southern Portugal, experiencing the peaceful serenity of the countryside and villages. It was difficult to realize that only a short distance away the poor country of Spain had been laid desolate after thirty-two months of civil war under the new dictator, Francisco Franco, and that the blood of her noble sons still flowed as the horrible internal revolution continued unabated.

From Portugal we traveled north into France, where the Full-Gospel revival had sprung up in 1930 led by Brother D. R. Scott and his wife, who were also our hosts for our entire time in that land. Brother Scott began his first French campaign in Le Havre with ten men in attendance, three of whom received healings—one for a mutilated wrist, which God healed instantly. France, at the time, was ripe for revival. Brother Carter and I found the French people very open to the Full-Gospel message of power. We ministered in Paris, Rouen, Marseilles, Lille, and also in the principality of Monte Carlo. The French are famous for their enjoyment of life, and good food and good wine are an important part of everyday living for almost all Frenchmen. But we saw a tremendous move of God in France, and the people of this predominantly Catholic land seemed to have a greater-than-usual faith.

In January and February of 1939, we held evangelistic crusades in Switzerland—Geneva, Vevey, Lausanne, Bern, Burgdorf, and Aarau. While in Aarau our host apologized for my having to sleep in the castle, because he didn't have accommodations for two. For hundreds of years, throughout the Middle Ages, the castles in these European countries served as fortresses. During the last century, a Swiss general had bought this particular castle and left it to his daughter, who was our hostess. We learned that when she died it would eventually become a museum.

My hostess led me up the steep, worn, and winding stairs into the tower. Everything creaked—from the ancient, heavy, oak doors on their squeaky, rusty hinges to the musty, antique furniture. There was no electricity, only flickering candlelight. She took great delight in graphically describing for me the bloody scenes enacted there during the castle's centuries of history. I got goose bumps on my goose bumps. I had the feeling that the place was haunted. There were unfamiliar noises, and I found getting to sleep a bit difficult, to say the least.

From Aarau we traveled to Zurich, Saint Gallen, and Schaffhausen. Switzerland was everything the travel folders make it out to be. With its beautiful, snow-capped mountains and freedom-loving people, we felt blessed and privileged to be there. Villages cling to steep mountain slopes in the Swiss Alps, and we were enchanted with the picturesque beauty wherever we turned.

Then it was back to England, where I was able to pioneer three churches that are still going today. I would rent a hall and conduct a crusade, assisted by a talented young musician. We advertised the crusades with handbills and ads in the newspapers. The meetings were blessed with marvelous conversions and healings, but my American preaching style was not always appreciated. One woman told me, "You know, Mr. Sumrall, God isn't deaf. You are yelling too loudly!"

In 1939, Europe was gearing up for World War II. It was not a safe place to be for those who lived there, nor for Americans like myself. I had become friendly with the British intelligence service, which frequently stopped to check up on me. As the war intensified, I was finally notified by British authorities that Americans with temporary visas should prepare to leave. The Germans were invading Holland and France, Poland had already been overrun, and England was atremble. Howard Carter was a British citizen, and he remained with his Bible school. I had no choice but to return to America.

Brother Carter and I had been like Paul and Timothy—an older man and a younger man—and we'd had the joy of traveling through many nations, preaching the Word, laying hands upon the sick, and seeing thousands receive the baptism of the Holy Spirit. It was difficult to leave this man whom I had come to love and admire so very much. We did not know if we would ever see each other again. War clouds hovered low over Great Britain, and no one knew what would happen next. But we did know that one day we would spend all eternity together, magnifying and praising the Lord with all the saints.

I took a freight ship back to the United States. The war was on.

15

A Long Arctic Winter

In South Bend, Indiana, in the autumn of 1940, while the war raged in Europe, I heard a missionary to Alaska speak. He wept as he related how difficult it was to reach these rough, tough people who often lived in debauchery. He said it was the hardest place in the world to win souls. That's all I needed. "I'll come," I told the missionary; and I went, spending the entire winter season in that last frontier land.

George Mueller, a great man of faith, is known to have said "Remember it is the very time for faith to work when sight ceases. The greater the difficulties, the easier for faith; as long as there remain certain natural prospects, faith does not get on as easily as where natural prospects fail." I would need to lean heavily on my faith in that rugged land.

I took the train to Seattle, then boarded the S.S. *Princess Norah* for the passage to Alaska. The Inland Passage is one of the most beautiful marine corridors in the world, with its chain of heavily wooded isles holding back the boisterous Pacific. One evening the Irish captain and I were pacing the aft deck, talking about Christianity. "What do you think of Christ?" I asked him. "Whose son is He?"

Removing his pipe from his mouth, the captain dramatically pointed it toward the blinking stars. "Those stars are my god, sir," he answered in a firm voice. "They have done more for me than anything of which I know. Since I was a small boy I have lived on the high seas, and night after night those wonderful stars have guided my boat. They have never led me astray. To me they are the most beautiful sight in the world. I admire them deeply; perhaps, even worship them."

"But who made your sparkling gods up there?" I asked him. "Who organized and who superintends their functions to guarantee that they stay in their orbits and remain faithful to you?"

"I do not know," he said, "and I'm not sure anyone else knows either."

As the captain leaned over the rail and watched the wake ripple in the moonlight, I said, "Captain, my God made your gods."

On my way through British Columbia, I stopped in the city of Prince Rupert for a week of special meetings. There the pastor informed me that on the day I was to leave I would be missing by a few hours the arrival of a young missionary serving with the Pentecostal Assemblies of Canada. Her name was Miss Louise Layman, and she was coming to tell them about work in the Argentine. Her name lodged in my thinking, and I had the fleeting thought that it would be nice to meet a young, single, woman missionary.

I discovered that Alaska is no longer a land of long-bearded sourdoughs with a lust for gold in their eyes; neither is it just a howling Arctic wilderness of frigid desolation. Modern Alaska has superseded frontier Alaska; and in 1940 it was a vigorous, aggressive, and challenging place to be.

I found out that only six states in the continental United States have as many commercial airfields. Fairbanks, the metropolis of the interior of Alaska, was the nerve-center for aviation. From there pilots known as the "northern eagles" fly over some of the most difficult and dangerous terrain in the world. Monoplanes are flown west to Nome, north to Point Barrow, east over the Yukon to Juneau, and south to the Aleutians with the nonchalance of a ten-minute pleasure jaunt over the city. In the winter months they replace the wheels of their planes with skis and use the far northern rivers for landing fields.

During the month of February, I visited the town of Nome on the Seward Peninsula in the Bering Sea. Nome was frozen in for the winter with about 125 miles of ice at its front door. The only means of outside communication was the airplane.

As I boarded the monoplane for Fairbanks, the pilot seated me in the cockpit alongside himself so that I could take pictures. Soon after we roared over the silent Arctic village and turned toward the vast, treeless tundra, the pilot sighted a fine herd of reindeer—possibly five or six hundred of them—to the north of us. "Hang on," he shouted, "we'll dip low over them so you can get some good pictures." He turned the plane and swooped low, and I got some great pictures. It was a rare thrill to see them running like that in their natural habitat.

Alaskan pilots realize the danger of lost minutes in midwinter when darkness is a great enemy, so it was all over very quickly. As we started for home after circling the reindeer, the pilot related exciting instances when he had seen packs of wolves attacking deer. We flew along in silence, and then he said, "Lester, we're lost. If we can locate the Koyukuk River, we might possibly find a small Indian village and land on the river."

Fear gripped my throat and I couldn't answer. I gazed out into the semidarkness at the undulating mounds of ice and snow. Was this to become a bleak, frozen grave for us? I began to pray.

After what seemed a long time, we sighted the winding curve of ice below us. The pilot recognized the river and turned the plane south, flying low as he looked for the twinkling lights of some fishing village. I silently thanked the Lord. At long last he sighted a few lights reflecting on the snow around some snow-covered log huts. The villagers heard the roaring plane and, since they know that ordinarily in Alaska no one flies at night, they rushed out with lanterns and stood along the edge of the river to give us light in our attempt to land on the ice. The first time our plane hit the ice, it must have bounced fifty feet into the air. Only our safety belts kept us from going right through the top of the plane. Another attempt was made; and though we bounced terribly, we straightened out and finally came to a halt. We taxied over the rough ice to the village, secured the plane, covered the engine with a tarpaulin, and put a small gas stove under it to keep it from freezing. We bunked with the local postmaster/storekeeper for the night.

In Alaska, to land safely in the dark is a miracle. To

land safely in the dark near an isolated village in mid-winter is a greater miracle. I have often thought of those people holding their lanterns high. What would we have done without their help? Isn't that a picture of what we, as Christians, need to do in this dark, sinful world?

The next morning we were able to gas up and take off, arriving in Fairbanks within the hour.

In Fairbanks I preached in the largest public hall available. Since I had recently returned from Russia and Nazi Germany, I spoke prophetically and very strongly against their anti-God philosophies and actions. I related what we had seen—the closing of churches and schools and the takeover of businesses. I spoke of the anti-Semitic hatred and my fear of what would happen to the Jews. I expressed concern about the welfare of our Christian brothers and sisters in these countries. Suddenly, four or five men in the meeting hall became very angry, scraping their feet on the floor, knocking over chairs, and stomping loudly out of the hall.

I felt strange about this—something sinister was in their actions—and the next morning I went to the local FBI office and reported it. I was told that they were, in fact, trying to locate some Nazis because their operations were being radioed across the North Pole to Germany. If Nazi Germany ever decided to attack America, it could very well come across the North Pole. They were seeking a way to trap those Nazis and asked me if I would cooperate.

"In what way?" I asked.

"Preach another sermon just as strong, and announce in the newspaper that you are going to preach about Hitler and Nazi Germany."

That's what I did. And sure enough, the next Sunday

night the same men showed up, scraping their feet on the floor, yelling out loud, calling me names, and eventually knocking over several chairs as they stomped loudly out the door. To my amazement the FBI man I had talked to scraped his feet on the floor, yelled at me, and knocked over chairs along with the Nazis. But the next day he called me from his office and said, "When we got outside, the Germans took me as a friend over to their headquarters. Now we have seven of them in custody. Thank you for your cooperation."

It was a long Arctic winter, but I was used by the Lord to open up new churches in Ketchikan, Fairbanks, and Anchorage. All three of these are strong churches today. It was my great joy to speak in many villages and cities in Alaska. I spoke in high schools, lectured at the University of Alaska, and preached as far north as Wiseman, seventy miles north of the Arctic Circle, and as far west as Nome, on the Bering Sea. My heart and soul were full of rich experiences and lifelong memories in the spring of 1941 as I came south out of that frigid air. The Lord once again had truly blessed.

Passing Prince Rupert, I stopped for a few meetings and then took the primitive railroad through the interior of British Columbia to Terrace, Smithers, Prince George, and beautiful Jasper National Park. In each town the Christians spoke of the missionary from the Argentine and of the rich blessing she had been to them. This made me curious to know this intrepid young adventuress who dared to visit these outposts of civilization in the northland, where typically only courageous and zealous male missionaries offer their services. I think my admiration for her was born at that time, and I wondered if there was some way I could catch up with her somewhere along the way.

16

South of the Border

Suddenly, violently, and without warning, the United States was thrust into World War II with the bombing of Pearl Harbor on December 7, 1941, by the Japanese. As a concerned citizen I rushed down to enlist in the Navy, volunteering my services as a chaplain. I was told there were enough men to fill the chaplaincy. With this, I re-packed my bags and headed south of the border. Latin America was my destination. The world was at war, but I would be fighting another type of battle with an unseen, but nonetheless real, enemy—the very enemy of all our souls.

I passed through Mexican immigration and customs at Juarez on the Rio Grande, then went overland via the Pan American Highway to tour every country of Central and South America from Mexico to the cataracts of Iguasu in the Argentine.

There were twenty nations in Latin America encom-passing eight million square miles—almost three times the size of the United States—and I wanted to see it all. Latin America has the longest mountain range in the world—

the Andes, which runs about four thousand miles from the Caribbean to Cape Horn. And there are three tremendous rivers—the Amazon in the center (the world's largest, deepest, and second longest), the Orinoco in the north, and the Plata in the south. In the center of the continent is the world's largest tropical forest, much of it unexplored by modern man. Map in hand, I looked at this vast territory and promised God that, with His help, I'd be faithful in preaching, teaching, healing, and helping needy souls wherever He would send me.

Mexico City was swarming with hordes of shoeshine boys whose eager ambition, I learned, was to become famous bullfighters in glittering clothes and get their pictures on the front page of newspapers and magazines. They needed Jesus; and while my shoes were being shined, I did my best to communicate to them that there was something better than becoming famous as a bullfighter. Our neighbors to the south presented a fascinating variety of colors, sights, and sounds. The culture took some getting used to; but by now I had become an inveterate traveler, and I knew how to be adaptable.

Here again I was confronted with the fact that nearly all of Mexico's people are Roman Catholic. The ancient architecture was related chiefly to their religion, and I learned much by studying some of their literature. There were, it seemed, thousands of impressive Catholic churches; but the poverty of the people seemed in stark contrast to these buildings.

Sports are popular in Mexico, and I was intrigued with their game of *jai alai* (which resembles handball), as well as with their cockfights and the bullfighting.

In Mexico I looked upon pyramids larger than those of

Egypt and wondered why more Americans didn't know about them. I visited the Otomi Indians in the jungles of Mexico, and the descendants of the Aztecs. I went to see Pericutin, a new volcano that had recently, without warning, erupted from a cornfield and buried an entire town, its cinder cone already four hundred feet high and still growing.

Like Paul, I adapted my ways to those of my hosts. I learned to be abased and to abound, while eating from a stew pot containing an ostrich—beak, feathers, toes, and entrails—with the Indians of the Gran Chaco Boreal.

Just south of Mexico is Guatemala where, in the city of Esquipulas, I visited the great cathedral containing the statue of the Black Christ, beyond contradiction the most "miraculous" image in the entire nation. The public was permitted to see it only at certain times each year, as it was kept in a sacred place, hidden beneath expensive coverings. It was commonly rumored among devotees that the image possessed flesh and blood and that anyone who touched it would die.

I learned that the Guatemalans' ancestors, the Maya Indians, built a highly developed civilization hundreds of years before Christopher Columbus discovered America. Market days in Guatemala are busy and colorful, but I discovered that Sunday is often their busiest market day. Guatemala is known for its rich coffee grown along the southern edge of the broad, central, mountainous region.

Almost all Guatemalans belong to the Roman Catholic church, but the Indians also follow many religious practices from their pre-Christian past. They worship local gods and spirits along with God, Jesus Christ, the Virgin

Mary, and their local patron saint. I found Indians praying to certain natural features in the hills representing various gods at planting and harvesting times.

Moving on down into El Salvador, missionary Perry Dymond met me with horses and an invitation to preach for six weeks in the hamlets of the mountainous wilderness of Honduras, at the time considered the most backward country of the Americas. It was the rainy season. The tropical jungle seemed impenetrable, but we climbed the steep, tortuous trails on muleback, and I was thankful for my experience doing much the same in China. Here were the hideouts of vicious jaguars, wild boar, brilliantly colorful wild turkeys, and monkeys, some of which we saw and others of which we heard bawling in the distance. We saw the magnificent ruins of Copan, the remains of the Mayan civilization, with amazing and massive stone work predating any established chronology in the New World.

It was almost dark when we came into view of the hamlet named Las Delicias (The Delicious), a string of about a half-dozen houses. I wondered where the congregation would come from. But I needn't have wondered. By 7:30 that night, the place where we met was packed with men and women.

The church was in the house of Señor Gutierrez. It was constructed of bamboo sticks plastered over with mud—a typical dwelling. This church came into being when Gutierrez, dying with a high fever, heard the salvation message and accepted the Lord as his Savior. He was not only saved, but also healed. He had been so close to death that his family and friends had made his coffin. When he was healed, he took the coffin and hung it on the rafters of the room that he then made into the gospel hall. There it hung—a silent testimony to the power of God. At the time I met him he was seventy years old but a robust and vigorous man, staunch in his faith and a dynamic witness to the miracle-working power of God.

I stood behind an improvised box-pulpit at one end of the room, which was about twelve by twenty-one feet, facing a circular board seat around the walls and some rough, backless seats in the middle. The only light consisted of a tin can with a rag for a wick, producing more smoke than light. The mountain people began to arrive about a half-hour before the meeting was to begin. Some had walked as far as eight miles. The place was so packed that there wasn't room for them all. Outside I could hear them singing heartily.

Long afterward I was to remember the scene—a mud hut on the side of a tropical mountain, the preacher and interpreter dressed in riding breeches and boots, and the congregation clothed in homemade garments, listening intently. There were very few children—maybe two out of every ten born survived the filthy environment and the lack of proper nourishment.

At the close of that service, these grateful people lighted large pieces of pine and started the long, dangerous trek back through the dense forest to their homes, the blazing light keeping the animals away and providing light for their feet on the pathway. I can still see them leaving in my mind's eye as I write this—single file along the mountain path, singing the songs of Zion. I am reminded of Psalm 119:105: "Thy word is a lamp unto my feet, and a light unto my path."

We concluded it was too cold in the high mountains to sleep in our hammocks; the best place to spend the night would be in the corn crib, a building made of bamboo canes and located in the yard. Perry, his wife, three children, and I went into the crib to make the best of it. When we rolled into our blankets—clothes, boots, and all—I was obliged to sleep carefully, for a few feet away in my corner a mother hen was sitting on a nest of eggs.

The roosters noisily woke us at the break of dawn. We climbed out of our bed rolls, refreshed ourselves by splashing ice cold water on our hands and faces from a gourd, and joined our host in his house. Breakfast was tortillas and black beans cooked over a primitive mud fireplace with no chimney in a dark and exceedingly dirty room. Then we saddled our mules, bade a final farewell to these friends, and took the narrow trail again to travel to the next mud church in the next mud village some five hours away. This experience was typical of the many my interpreter and I had in the weeks ahead as we traveled from one isolated place to another.

Moving farther south I came into Nicaragua, the largest country of Central America, my destination being El Sauce (not too far inland from the Honduran border). The Protestant church had never ventured to advance into this Roman Catholic stronghold, which was a shrine center for the entire nation. Pilgrims journey to this point from many parts of Central America to see another replica of the Black Christ that is supposed to perform miracles.

The story, as I heard it, was that itinerant priests long ago traveled throughout the countries of Central America with these replicas to bring "blessings" to the people and to collect money for the mother church. The padre in charge of the one in El Sauce died. The church authorities sent another padre to bring the image back home but he, too, died. All then came to the conclusion that this Black Christ wished to reside in El Sauce. I was told that on certain annual feast days the crowds have been so immense that pilgrims have been crushed to death by the throng in the cathedral that houses this idol.

The people in this part of the country were unusually fanatical, making it dangerous for Protestants at times. I met Victor Mendoza, a feisty, five-foot, dynamic, one-time revolutionary who came into contact with the Bible, eagerly read it, accepted Christ as his personal Savior, and embraced Protestantism. Possessing a natural gift for public speaking, he progressed quickly as a lay Christian, revealing his integrity before the world and the church. He went away to the Bible school in Santa Ana, El Salvador, for ministerial training and returned to his native Nicaragua to win victories for Christ.

Victor possessed fearless faith, seemingly thriving on trouble. His countrymen roared at him, "Fanatic!" "Heretic!" "Demon!" But he continued in the work he felt God had called him to do. He chided the people for worshiping pieces of painted clay and inanimate wood. He told of his experience with the Roman church and its intrigues. So persuasive was he, and so powerful was the movement of the Holy Spirit in this courageous man, that people from all over came to hear him preach.

From this mixed multitude Victor Mendoza soon built a thriving church that became one of the largest Protestant strongholds in the country. In many respects this little man with the big heart reminded me of the apostle Paul. But he was restless and knew that God hadn't called him to stay in one place. He became a pioneer for the faith in that far corner of the world—preaching, teaching, baptizing, and zealously contending for the faith.

It was encounters such as this with reborn Latin Americans—the result of "seeds" planted during the past one hundred years of evangelical missions in that country—that spurred me on. Not only was this land beautiful and historic, but I found it to be a place of incalculable possibilities for evangelization.

17

Into the Heart of the Great South American Continent

Place your finger on a map on the Tropic of Capricorn, running directly through the center of South America at sixty degrees west longitude, and you will be touching the heart of the great South American continent. As the eagle flies, it is about eighteen hundred miles north to the Caribbean Sea, off Venezuela, and another eighteen hundred miles south to Tierra del Fuego, off Argentina. To the east of that geographical position it is about seven hundred miles to the enormous expanses of the Atlantic waters, and to the west seven hundred miles to the tranquil bosom of the Pacific.

In this vast Gran Chaco heart of South America live many tribes of the original men of this continent. They can correctly be called the "Forgotten Men," as they have been neglected by governments, charities, philanthropic societies, and most religious communions. They, with their brother tribes from the mighty Aztecs of Mexico to the Onas and Tehuelches of Patagonia, have suffered themselves to be *least*, *last*, and almost *lost*. I have never been confronted with more dire poverty and depressing human hopelessness than I found among these indigenous peoples of Latin America. What an eye-opening experience this was for me!

These people comprise an estimated 356 known tribes, many of them existing in a state of cannibalism and savagery. The Spanish found the Incas living in houses of granite; I found their descendants living in houses of mud. Once this proud race wore golden ornaments, but I saw the current residents of the area wearing copper and alloys like brass. This tragic economic deterioration of the red man has been brought about by his white "superiors," and much of it, shockingly and sadly, in the name of Christianity. I was appalled and grieved.

I crossed the Panama Canal into this South American continent and came into the country of Colombia. In the city of Sogamoso I met Olimpia de Lobo (Olimpia Wolf), the cherished daughter of a prominent Colombian sculptor, herself an artistic genius. At one time she was one of the most ardent Catholics in the city, known for her beautiful art objects and for her work retouching and repairing the images that so many Catholics worship. Observers often commented that she had placed a divine loveliness in the countenance of the saints; and she would respond, "Yes, and so they are divine."

The devotion of this Columbian woman to her church was admirable. I have not encountered many people in my worldwide travels who get up at five o'clock, go to church, and pray. Later in the morning she would retrace her steps to the church altar to offer her prayers to the various saints and spend another one-and-a-half hours in such devotion. The first Friday of each month she would take a special communion, and in her home holy lamps burned before pictures of Mary and Christ. These lamps were not extinguished for ten years, when this talented and devoted woman came in contact with the Bible.

All the religious ceremony, the pomp and glory of the church, did not satisfy the heart of this artist. She longed intensely for something she did not possess, and the sorrows of her heart were many. The prayers and rituals became tiresome, and she sought elsewhere for the peace her heart was demanding. At first she purchased books on spiritism (as many Latin Americans do) and began to study them. But her soul whispered to her that spiritism was false. When she held the Bible in her hands and opened it, from the very first verse it gripped her soul. Avidly she read the Book from cover to cover and began to pray, "Lord, put me among Your chosen ones."

The day came when the Wegners, veteran Presbyterian missionaries, came to the Sogamoso district (where a million people lived, but no missionary had been established); and refined Olimpia de Lobo found herself among these "chosen ones." Another seven years were to go by, however, before Señora de Lobo recognized the truth of Isaiah 44:22: "I have blotted out, as a thick cloud, thy transgressions, and, as a cloud, thy sins: return unto me; for I have redeemed thee." Inexpressible joy filled the soul of this artist when she realized that she was really redeemed—God had said so! For the first time in her life she had the true assurance of her conversion. Then she was directed to read verses 9 and 10 in this same chapter:

They that make a graven image are all of them vanity; and their delectable things shall not profit; and they are their

131

own witnesses; they see not, nor know; that they may be ashamed. Who hath formed a god, or molten a graven image that is profitable for nothing?

God was speaking to her from His Word. She went to the table and blew out her "holy lamps" on the family altar. She burned her many "holy" books and kept only her Bible. Then she rid her home of pictures of saints, charms, scapulas, written prayers, and the small statues that had been so much a part of her life for so long. She cried out to God, "Lord, forgive me for being an idolatress. I did it in ignorance. Now I shall have no altar but my heart, and there Christ shall be my Priest."

Encounters such as this strengthened my resolve to help and encourage the missionaries and lay men and women I was privileged to meet. Precious souls such as Señora de Lobo needed to hear the message of redemption.

Then it was on to Peru, where I met survivors of the horrendous glacial flood of fifty-foot waves coming down from Huascaran, at 22,205 feet the highest peak in the Peruvian Andes. The flood had destroyed the city of Huaras with its fifteen thousand inhabitants. When I was there, six months later, the authorities were still finding pieces of the bodies of the dead.

I learned of the persecution and stoning of the first evangelical missionaries to the area. Then I heard of the miraculous protection afforded many of them during the flood and saw where God literally divided the waters around the homes of those who prayed directly to Him for safety. The water, I was told, plunged right through the Avenida Raimondi, a beautiful, eucalyptus-lined prom-enade where not a tree or sprig of grass remained—only ghastly, sepulcher-white stones—making the place look like a cemetery.

I met Dr. Walter Manuel Montano, called the "Mountain Man" of Peru. He told me the most amazing story of his escape from the Roman Catholic priesthood. Convinced of the validity of evangelical Protestantism, he sought to leave the Catholic church. But they considered him a heretic, he told me, so he was held as a prisoner in a monastery in Lima for six years before escaping. After that, he said, he felt he was in constant danger, because he heard that someone in the church had offered plenary indulgence to anyone who would kill him. At one point he was captured and thrown into a filthy dungeon. He was finally convicted of attempting to overthrow the Peruvian government (a trumped-up charge) and deported from the country. He came to this country and, interestingly, married a young woman from my brother's church in Chicago. Later he proved his mountain strength and courage by returning to Peru, the place where he was most hated and persecuted, and took up his life's work in propagating the gospel of Jesus Christ.

Defying the power of Rome and the Peruvian government in his stand for religious liberty, he became pastor of the First Peruvian Evangelical Church of Lima, where I had the privilege of conducting union meetings of all evangelicals of the city. This was a rich experience; there were many others in different places with God's chosen ones.

Paraguay is a small, landlocked republic in the heart of South America. Here, in Asunción, the primitive capital, we traveled by train and then horseback to a wilderness leper-asylum—seven thousand acres of lovely, forested hills and valleys—to visit the most forlorn folk in the world. These were outcasts from society, plagued with this cancerous disease, living without any comforts of life to cheer them in their slow but inevitable death.

Missionary Albert Widner and I had been invited by a Mr. Normant, pastor of the International Church of Asuncion, to visit the Santa Isabel Leper Colony and preach to those desolate people. Inside the entrance gate we saw some eighty huts in which lived a community of 370 persons—not all of them lepers, but husbands, wives, and children living together, with and without leprosy. Of course, children are born in the colony, and they usually have to stay there as there is no other provision for them. It was indescribably sad to see boys and girls having no trace of leprosy being reared in this undesirable environment. How my heart ached for them—I would have scooped them up in my arms and taken them back with me if it had been at all humanly possible. Three of those fine, intelligent little boys, with no evidence whatsoever of leprosy, ran to us, took our horses to water, and later turned them out to pasture.

The visitor must make the first advances of friendliness, as the lepers naturally feel that everyone is afraid of contracting their disease. So we made the rounds, greeting them personally. How can I describe what we saw? Next to the missionary's hut was the leper hospital where the advanced cases stayed, awaiting death. In it we found thirteen cots with creatures on them who defy verbal or written description. Their faces were badly deformed; some of their noses had already been broken off, and others had perforations in their faces through which putrid matter oozed. Their legs and feet were in terrible condition, some

134

of them resembling the hoof of a horse and covered with malignant sores. Their hands were badly deformed, the thumb seeming to sink back into the hand and the fingers paralyzed.

Their huts were filthier than any charitable institution I had ever seen—and some of them can be deplorably bad. They contained no floors, and little furniture. Pieces of fresh meat were hanging from the wall or tied to the foot of the bed to be cooked the following day. As I looked up in one place, I saw a hole in the straw roof through which the rain came.

As for the lepers, their clothing and bedding were rotting with filth. They begged for clothing, but we were unable to help them since we traveled so lightly ourselves. The missionary informed us that when blankets and sheets were given to them, they often sold them in order to obtain food.

The only sanitary convenience was a primitive privy in the backyard. Small tin pans were provided for their bathing; but there was no free laundry service, which explained why so many of them were dirty—they could not wash their own clothing or bedding.

Our next stop was the colony jail. Most of these lepers were not Christians; this explained the need for a jail. Shortly before our arrival, one leper had shot another, and this was not too uncommon. The colony had six policemen, all lepers. One of them, the chief, was allowed to carry a gun.

I was amazed to see men from all stations of life living in this colony. The first man we met had been a prominent man of the world; now he was forgotten. He had been editor of three newspapers, a popular labor leader, and had been sent to Rome and Moscow as a delegate representing labor unions. But his skin became insensitive—the telltale mark of early leprosy—and soon the ulcers appeared along with gross disfiguration of his earlobes, hands, and feet. The government police, in a cleanup raid, dispatched him to the leper asylum. He was the most dignified and the cleanest leper in the colony and could make a guest feel at home even in a leper den.

Another leper was a politician; we found a schoolmaster, four expert wood craftsmen, a tailor, a dressmaker, and many other skilled workers. The first lepers built their huts of mud; but those huts were being replaced with better ones, as the professional carpenters were willing to work for the good of the community when it was possible for the missionary to supply them with tools and materials.

More than a hundred lepers came to our service. I looked out at those despairing individuals living with a death sentence hanging over them, waiting for some words of hope in their hopeless situation. It was difficult to keep from weeping as a group of the lepers sang the Spanish rendering of "Our Home over There." I poured out my heart to them, giving them glorious, life-giving words from the gospel of Christ. I could feel our hearts united; and when the appeal was given, many came forward for prayer. I regretted that we could not shake hands with these lepers or put our arms around them—you could feel that they needed and wanted this, too, but it was forbidden.

When we left, we had fifteen kilometers to ride by horseback before we could reach the train station, and then we had a ten-hour train ride ahead of us. Some of the lepers gathered to say good-bye early that next morning, and as we rode away we heard "Hasta la vista" (until we meet again). We took the road back to civilization, to friends and to the comforts of life; but they remained behind to suffer alone and remain the forgotten ones—until we would meet again where leprosy never comes.

My diary reminds me of the many interesting sights I saw in these countries. Tin mines were pointed out to us and Inca ruins displaying masonry more remarkable than any I had seen in London or Paris. We saw llama herds high in the Andes Mountains in Peru. Throughout the country, from time to time, we saw breathtaking vistas and beautiful rivers, waterfalls, and lakes. Wherever we went, I was intrigued by the people; and always their faces looked familiar. These, too, were the people I had seen in my vision as a young man.

Buenos Aires, Argentina, is one of the finest cities in the world, the third largest in the Western Hemisphere. Here, as elsewhere, I found that each Latin American country and city has its own national customs, but most of them were based on Spanish and Portuguese rules of conduct and manners.

We came flying into Rio de Janeiro, Brazil, from the south by Panagra Airways and witnessed below us the world's most beautiful harbor. In this great city I was met by a Brazilian jeweler, Adalberto Arrais, whom I had met six years previously when Howard Carter and I were in that city. Here was a jeweler by trade who accepted Christ and found Him to be the pearl of great price. I met another interesting young man, Paulo Lobo, who was called the "King of Football" by his countrymen. He had a remarkable conversion experience and was foreman of a coffee company owned by his father. He was being used mightily by God to lead his workers to the Lord. These and other evangelicals warmly welcomed my interpreter and me, and the time spent in that great city was profitable for the Lord Jesus Christ.

By December 1942, I had preached from Alaska at the top of the world to Argentina at the bottom, not omitting a single country en route. (This book has only covered some of those travels, of course.) But added to my burden for souls was the sad news from home that my sister Leona had been stricken with incurable, crippling muscular dystrophy. With this heavy on my heart, I crossed the immense Andes by train under the shadow of Mt. Aconcagua, standing thirty-three thousand feet into the heavens, from Chile, to the lovely city of Mendoza, Argentina, where once again I heard of Miss Louise Layman and the blessing she was to all the saints. Then, at a wedding in Buenos Aires, we came face-to-face. She smiled and I smiled. That encounter was to change my life forever.

The author at age 17.

The author, seated in the center on the left of Howard Carter (with beard and bow tie), in Wilma, Poland, in March 1936.

On mule back in Tibet.

Speaking in an early evangelistic service.

Bethel Temple, Manila, under construction in 1952.

Lester and Louise on their wedding day, September 30, 1944.

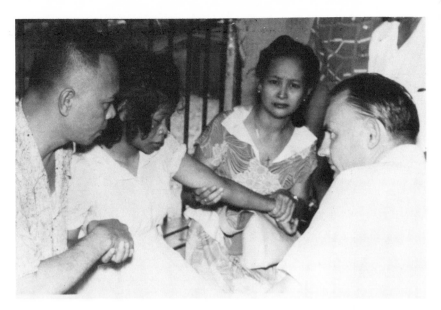

Clarita Villanueva in Bilibid prison, Manila. Her deliverance sparked a revival in 1953.

A revival service in Manila.

Lester and Louise visit children from the first orphanage in Baguio, the Philippines.

The Sumralls at the groundbreaking for radio station WHME-FM, South Bend, in 1968.

Cornerstone-laying service for Christian Center Church in 1968.

The Sumralls on the first broadcast of "Today with Lester Sumrall" from WHMB-TV, Indianapolis, in 1972.

18

Wedding Bells

It was on a typically Latin day, in a setting in harmony with what one envisions a wedding day to be, that I met the future Mrs. Lester Sumrall. She was playing the bridal march on the organ. As the bride and bridegroom took their places at the altar, I looked toward the organist, and she looked across at me. At that moment we smiled at each other.

Later, on the patio where the wedding dinner was to be served, I observed her again happily decorating the tables. The patio was shadowed with luxuriant flora, and the sun streaming through the foliage made golden shafts on the flowered mosaic-tiled floor. I was delighted when I saw the lovely organist sitting across the table from me and we were finally introduced. When I learned that this was Miss Louise Layman, the missionary from Canada, I mused, "So this is the woman I've been hearing about from the top of the world to the bottom!"

I wasted no time in telling her that in my many travels, regardless where I went, it seemed that she was well thought of and that she had left a trail of blessing. We had many mutual friends and discovered much common ground on which to converse. She asked me if I had visited Prince Rupert and later told me she could tell from the "light in my eyes" that I had enjoyed the beautiful, rugged Northland. We enjoyed speaking of places and people we both had visited and knew. She told me she had anticipated meeting me also as she had seen brochures with my picture and notes on my travels, and she had heard about me in British Columbia when we had missed meeting each other by only a few hours (when I was on my way to Alaska). I was able to tell her that I admired her even before I knew her.

Our second meeting was on Christmas day at the mission station in Henderson, a town about seven hours by train from Buenos Aires. It was Louise's home station, and I had gone there to minister. I was pleasantly surprised to find a gaily wrapped parcel under a Christmas tree with my name on it. I opened it and found a little wooden burro with wheels under his feet. When in motion, his hips went up and down in a comical fashion. Louise had given me my first present! I promptly named the donkey *Luisa* ("Louise" in Spanish). A few days later, while in the home of a missionary where there was a small child, I gave the burro away.

From Henderson I traveled up the Plata and Paraguay rivers to Asunción, Paraguay, then on to the Church of England mission among the Lengua-Moscoy Indians of the Gran Chaco Boreal. Riding on horseback for more than three weeks and on primitive river boats, I had plenty of time to meditate on recent meetings and acquaintances and write notes of appreciation for hospitality received and fellowship enjoyed. Thus began my correspondence with Louise, which continued for better than a year.

We each appreciated the labors of the other, and we found that we had much in common: We were born the same year, the same month, and only eleven days apart. We both accepted Christ as personal Savior while in our teens and promptly offered our lives to Christian ministry. We ministered to congregations as resident ministers while still in our teens. From the time of our conversion, we each desired to do missionary work in foreign lands; and we departed North America for mission fields in the same month of the same year—she from New York to Argentina, and I from San Francisco to New Zealand and Australia.

Eventually I proposed marriage to Louise and she accepted. It was all done by mail, of course. The day I received her reply, I made this entry in my diary:

> I am engaged today! One month and three days after I wrote my proposal, the answer was received. Sitting here in the great Pan American air terminal in Mexico City, waiting for the plane to take me to Tuxpan where I shall go back and visit the Otomi Indians, I read again the letter received this morning from Louise, forwarded to me from my home in Chicago. She has consented to leave the Argentine and return home to Canada where we shall be married later this year. May God unite our lives to do a great work for Him in every part of the world. She said she had prayed about the matter for a week and had consulted her senior missionaries on the field—that is a good spirit. The long string is about to knot! My heart feels certain she will make a fine companion as she is the choice of God, and my choice. The distance is so great and the war re-

strictions and censorships so slow, it takes time for word to come and go. I trust the same censor read both letters and knows how it all came out!

I withdrew all the funds from my bank account, adding twenty-four dollars, and dispatched a draft by airmail to bring home the one I had chosen.

Louise had three months to prepare for departure from Argentina. When the long-awaited day for our third meeting arrived, I was both nervous and excited. I arrived at the international airport in New Orleans on schedule, but Louise's plane did not arrive and it wasn't until the following evening that her name appeared on the passenger list. Even then the immigration authorities would not release her until some American stood responsible for her crossing the States and entering Canada. Of course I was more than glad to take her off the immigration authorities' hands. We embraced, and I whisked her away in my green Hudson coupe.

Louise's home was in London, Ontario. The months between May and September will always be remembered in our lives. These were weeks of making memories, of building companionship that would brave the vicissitudes of missionary life, of becoming acquainted and talking over the future, and of planning for years of combined ministry. They became also a time of synchronizing two personalities into a harmonious whole, and we were both amazed at how our ideals ran parallel. We could see God's hand and His divine plan miraculously leading us in separate ways and now preparing to unite us in labor for Him.

September 30, 1944, was *the* day. It was one of those beautiful "Indian summer" afternoons, a perfect day for a wedding. At exactly 2:30 P.M. I stood facing the audience as the organ played the familiar strains of Lohengrin. I was a typical bridegroom—my pulse racing as I saw my bride walking down the white-carpeted aisle on the arm of her stepfather, the Rev. J. D. Saunders, and I added my gasp of appreciation to the other audible whispers of "Isn't she a beautiful bride!" My brother, the Rev. Ernest Sumrall, was my best man. Officiating was Dr. Wortman, missionary physician and uncle of the bride.

At the close of the ceremony, Mrs. Wortman sang "Together with Him." The last verse of that song was especially prophetic of the life we would live together:

Together with Jesus, constrained by His love,
We seek for the lost ones and point them above.
From valleys of service to mountains of rest
He guides us and keeps us; in Him we are blest.

Our union was pronounced, the wedding supper was celebrated, and farewells were said. Our Hudson roared away across the twilight of the lovely Ontario countryside, rich in its autumn colors, toward Niagara Falls, the honeymooners' haven.

19

A Fifty-Thousand-Mile Honeymoon

We had many invitations from churches across Canada and the United States to minister as a team in special services; instead, we followed the leading of our hearts. We both felt that as our lives had previously been devoted to missionary work, a missionary venture would be the only suitable honeymoon for us.

God proved to be our unfailing Guide and directed our travels from island to island and country to country even though, like the apostle Paul on his missionary journeys, we had no predetermined itineraries planned. The world was at war. Travel was extremely difficult. But the Lord always made the way when, humanly speaking, there was no way.

We started out through Quebec and New Brunswick into primitive Nova Scotia, with its miles of apple orchards, where ancient oxcarts laden with apples and other farm produce still lumber through the towns and villages. We stayed with poor, rural families who made makeshift beds for us in their kitchens near the stoves. We preached to the fishermen and their families. Nova Scotia has the most rugged coastline I have ever seen, and the people in these Maritime Provinces had been grossly neglected by most religious groups.

We arrived back in the United States for a great New Year's youth rally in Detroit. Then, while Roosevelt was being inaugurated for his fourth term, we were on our way to Puerto Rico, 1,150 miles south of Miami, touching down on the way in Spanish Cuba and French Haiti. We flew through one of the most severe tropical storms either of us had ever experienced. It was a real *tormenta*, and we prayed earnestly for safety.

In lovely, tropical Puerto Rico we visited indigenous churches, propagated and governed by their own people without the presence of even one resident missionary. We were happy to see that there was religious liberty on this island and that the voice of the minority was being heard.

The Latins are natural dramatists, and they excell in radio broadcasting. There were gospel programs on the radio every day, and several stations gave us free time to preach the gospel.

Living conditions among the poor of Puerto Rico were pitiful, and we found ourselves sleeping in houses infested with roaches, fleas, and bedbugs. The mosquitoes had no mercy and were like zooming jets! This was the saddest aspect of our long trip, for Louise contracted malignant malaria. An American-educated doctor held out little hope for my lovely bride, and I grieved and wept. But then I got down on my knees and prayed like I'd never prayed before, asking God to miraculously heal and strengthen her. And that's just what He did! We later were able to continue on our missionary journey, traveling through the

West Indies and South America, up the Amazon River for 1,100 miles where there are millions of mosquitoes; but there was never a recurrence of malaria. We rejoiced greatly for this deliverance.

We encountered spiritism in Puerto Rico, just as I had encountered it on a trip to Cuba some years before. I asked about its origins and was told that it came from Africa. The West Indies had ten million black people, descendants of the slaves. When the ancestors of these black populations were stolen from their homes in Africa and brought as slaves to the New World, they brought their superstitions, witchcraft, and demon worship with them. These became a curse to the Western world. The spiritism in Puerto Rico and Cuba, the voodooism of Haiti, the shangoism of Trinidad, the candomblé of Brazil—all had the same origin, but they were and are by no means limited to the black citizens of those places.

In Puerto Rico spiritism was and is a respected and established religion. Doctors, lawyers, and men and women in other professions are not ashamed of being recognized as members of the cults. We found the deadly doctrines of spiritism had found their way even into the high intellectual circles of the University of Puerto Rico. We were saddened to see vendors of religious articles selling spiritist goods at the same time. I stopped at a sidewalk vendor near a church and found he was selling printed prayers, holy pictures of saints, rosaries,and a book entitled *The Gospel According to Spiritism*. We were more convinced than ever that our work was cut out for us.

From the palm-lined coast of Puerto Rico, on board the S.S. *Prince Bernhard*, we crossed the blue waters of the Caribbean, touching at St. Thomas, then continuing on to St. Croix, the largest island in the Virgin group. The people were ultrasocial, and we found a ready audience for the gospel message. The old towns of Christianstad and Frederickstad made us feel we were living back in the eighteenth century.

We took a plane back to St. Thomas, the capital of the Virgin Islands. This was a lush, verdant island thirteen miles long and only a few miles wide. It is also historically significant, for on the hill overlooking the bay was Bluebeard's Tower, now a hotel. There the notorious pirate supposedly watched for merchant ships to pass so that he and his pirate comrades could plunder and capture the cargo. We preached in a mission where the islanders called out, "Yeah." "At'right." "Amen." "Sure." We found both islands overrun with small missions—predominantly European, a remnant of the once-Danish rule.

As we continued our way through the Antilles, the S.S. *Prince Bernhard* stopped at two of the Windward Islands, St. Lucia and Granada. We saw golden sunrises on an emerald sea—holding hands, enjoying each other's presence and the gift of love God had given to us. Those were memorable days.

We found an interesting native church in Granada. It was in the country, and the drive through the spice plantations and along the tropical sea was glorious. The house was full of natives who listened eagerly to two sermons. How wonderful it was to look from the church onto the Caribbean Sea and watch the silver path of the moon come directly toward us!

After preaching in the country and returning weary from the journey, we went aboard ship to spend the night.

147

The next day we sailed for Trinidad, the southernmost tip of the West Indies, just ten degrees north of the equator. The following morning we anchored in the flat, humid harbor of Port-of-Spain. Trinidad, discovered in 1496 by Columbus and named after the Trinity, we found to be one of the strangest cauldrons in the world—a romantic and historic playground of buccaneers and pirates, millionaries and paupers.

The walk down the main street of rustic, shabby Port-of-Spain was like taking a trip around the world. Africans predominate in this melting pot. They were brought over as slaves, and in 1838, the abolition of slavery set them free. But in this crucible of Trinidad life we found the Orient, Occident, and the African stewing together. Added to this we found the Afro-Chinese, Indo-Chinese, Eurasians, Latin Americans (mostly from Venezuela), and English—creating every shade in the racial spectrum.

The Hindus in Port-of-Spain, scarcely touched by the gospel, were living as they did in India, dressing in their quaint Indian garb and building heathen temples in which to worship grotesque images. They spoke so little English that we made little progress in communicating with them. They could not explain their religion to us, but one of their paintings depicted a woman with a serpent under her feet. We felt that this was a distorted story of redemption.

Neighbors of the heathen Hindus are the Africans, practicing their black arts. We saw fifty-three Islamic temples on the island. We asked the Muhammadan priest what his religion taught regarding Jesus Christ. "A great prophet, like Muhammad," he said. Then, as if confiding a great secret, he said that his holy books taught that Jesus was returning in the near future to be king of the earth.

"But," he shook his head and pulled at his short beard, "there is first to be a world revolution, when father will kill son and brother will kill brother, and out of that sorrow Jesus will appear as the World Savior and the World Ruler."

We asked him if he believed Jesus really died on the cross. He shook his head no, explaining that Jesus slipped through the hands of the mob on the day of the crucifixion and that in their fury they grabbed a man who looked like Jesus and crucified him instead. Then the priest laughed. "But, what happened to Jesus?" we asked.

"He slipped off to heaven while nobody was looking!"

We asked him what someone would have to do to join his religion. "We would welcome you to join the truth," he said. "Read the Koran, say you believe, then you are a Muslim."

We asked him to define sin. He responded, "There is no sin. Everything is good and has to be good. It is only wrong ideas that people have. There is no sin."

Our ministry in Trinidad was full and interesting. We spoke in churches, public halls, by radio, and at an American military camp, the great Waller Field Air Base. One of the more memorable aspects of our stay in Trinidad was that we celebrated our first wedding anniversary there at the air base. The missionaries, soldiers, and Christians on the island gave us a great anniversary day. I received a stuffed crocodile, and my wife was given a beautiful tray made of varicolored inlaid wood. We conducted meetings in the Prince's Building, the largest auditorium on the island. Then we went to the smaller towns, preaching in high school auditoriums and at the Presbyterian church. No experience was more exciting, however, than preaching to the convicts at His Majesty's Carrera Prison on an island in the Gulf of Paria across the channel from the mainland of Trinidad.

The water was calm and the massive rock fortress was impressive as we half-circled it to get to the private dock of the prison. We passed through great steel gates and made our way to a tropical porch where the prisoners were waiting. We were accompanied by a Nazarene missionary who led the prisoners in prayers and hymns. We observed the prisoners during this time carefully. They were a healthy, muscular group who looked like an average group of men, mainly black men and Oriental Indians. I spoke to them about the cross of Christ and its true meaning and power to the unconverted. A number of the men raised their hands in decision for salvation. At noon we left, returning to freedom; but as we descended the spiral stone stairs to the dock and waved good-bye to the guards, I understood more fully that "the way of transgressors is hard" (Prov. 13:15).

Leaving the island of Trinidad, we flew south toward the huge continent of South America. Almost immediately we were crossing the flood rivers of the Orinoco River basin, and we could see its tributaries making Egyptian-like hieroglyphics on the face of the earth. We first deplaned in British Guiana, a primitive-looking territory. Then it was on to Dutch Guiana, called Surinam, where we heard the natives speaking Takitaki, a combination of Dutch and English. Our last stop was in Cayenne, the capital of French Guiana, before crossing the equator to journey to our destination—Belem, Brazil.

The tropical storm crashed upon the Pan Am plane as we flew low over the raging Amazon River. It had been a pleasant journey until fifteen minutes before landing in Belem, when a torrential rainstorm broke upon us. The great plane trembled and shook as we came in for a landing. We were scheduled for ten busy days of meetings and were met by Señora Lydia Nelson and Pastor Pereiro. The national pastor asked if I was willing to begin speaking that night, and I told him I was. We had spoken in Trinidad on Sunday night, and by the marvel of air travel we spoke that Monday night in Brazil without feeling weary.

We were awakened at 6:00 A.M. by cannon shots. There had been talk of a revolution in the country, and our first thoughts were that perhaps it was under way. Later, at breakfast, it was explained that the largest religious fiesta of the year had begun and would continue for two weeks, including three Sundays. It was the nationals' annual feast to the Señora de Nazareth (Lady of Nazareth).

At 8:30 the first Sunday morning of the fiesta, a great procession began that lasted for many hours. First came Brazilian soldiers with a brass band and a miniature castle borne by a group of men. Following this were banners for Mary, statues of all sizes, and thousands of worshipers, the majority barefoot (evidence that they had made a special pledge to Mary). Almost everyone carried a present for the Virgin—pineapples, watermelons, shoes, candles, images, liquors, goats and other animals.

Along the sidewalk were liquor stands where nuns served drinks. Over the center of the two main streets was a huge image of Mary made of cardboard and studded with hundreds of electric lightbulbs. It was garish and our hearts were saddened by these sights and the bedraggled children, many of them wailing loudly, and the staggering drunk men and women. We were on our way to the church where we were holding services, knowing there were thousands who needed to hear the truth. At the close of that morning service, our hearts rejoiced to see those come forward who, after hearing the gospel, had found the true Light of the World.

We were the guests of missionary Nels Nelson, a Swedish-born pastor, and his wife. Their work was tremendous and his church had 3,700 baptized members. We enjoyed large crowds at all the services. Pastor Nelson kept a record of 140 persons who were counseled and accepted Christ during those ten days of meetings.

Realizing a dream come true, we flew eleven hundred miles up the Amazon River in an eleven-seater seaplane, over the widest and deepest water in the world, into the Brazilian jungles, the largest unbroken forest in the world. Five hours later we were in Manaos, in sweltering hot weather and a tropical cloudburst.

Manaos was once the Queen of Rubber, a hub of activity, but we found it to be a decaying city. Later we were to refer to it as moldly Manaos. Still, here, too, were people who needed to hear the truth. We spoke in two missions and estimated that 90 percent of the people we saw were undernourished and victims of malaria. They needed to hear a message of hope, and we urged upon them the need to continue to hope in God.

Contrary to rumors of "lost tribes," we found few Indians in the jungles; they were becoming extinct in many areas. And when Indians accept the "new religion," evangelical protestantism, they become outcasts of their tribes.

Since we had traveled by the "Baby Clipper" seaplane

into the interior of Amazonas, we desired to return by boat. We secured a much-coveted cabin on the S.S. *Virginia*, expecting a quiet voyage with few passengers. But, what a shock. The boat was jammed with everything from human beings to turtles, pigs, ducks, chickens, turkeys, twelve cows, two monkeys, a parrot, dogs, cats, and crates of fish. The decks were piled high with Brazilian goods—furniture of every description, chests of hardwood, large mattresses, rugs, suitcases, and trunks.

We were warned not to drink the water unless we used water purification tablets, and we had been warned not to eat the green vegetables. So we ate and drank sparingly and were happy to get off the ship in Belem once again where we ministered to the large congregation of Pastor Nelson.

Our work in the extreme north was now completed, and we could travel farther southward. Our itinerary was to take us to crusades in the Brazilian cities of Bahia, Rio de Janeiro, São Paulo, and Belo Horizonte. Our first stop was at Porte Alegre, halfway down the eastern seaboard of the South American continent. This was an exciting time, when God opened doors where there were seemingly no doors. We obtained a room in a hotel where there were long waiting lines; we were able to get two improvised, cushionless aisle seats on an ancient bus from São Paulo to Curitiba—a Ford V-8 motor hitting on six cylinders, stopping thirteen times for repairs over roads full of holes. From Itijai to Florianapolis we rode in the cab of a big olive-colored army truck hauling rice and beans to an army camp. We had Christmas Eve dinner in Rio de Janeiro, preaching in the open air on street corners as well as in enormous churches and rented buildings. Wherever we went—whether to lone individuals or to the masses —we witnessed to the love and mercy of Jesus Christ.

We made our way south overland through Uruguay, then to the Argentine, down to Bolivar and Henderson, where Louise had labored for eight years. Here we were especially warmly welcomed, and Louise and I reminisced about our second meeting there on Christmas Day in 1942.

We preached in La Plata, then from the airport in Mendoza flew over the majestic, snow-capped Andes to a meeting in Santiago, capital of the "Boot String Republic" of Chile. This was a union meeting of all evangelicals and was conducted in a Presbyterian church. Fourteen denominations participated, and it was beautiful to see everyone cooperating so harmoniously as one body in Christ.

From Santiago we flew to Lima, Peru, for the Easter season services at *La Victoria* Methodist Church. This was my third visit to Peru, but the first for Louise. We were there amid the usual parades in which the local religious sects carried statues depicting Mary as alive and Christ as dead. Our meetings presented Mary as dead and Christ as alive!

Our hearts rejoiced as we saw the church filled to overflowing and many standing. Many souls were added to the growing body of believers and the Protestant church in Latin America. The seed of the gospel had been sown in the byways of Peru by other faithful witnesses to Christ, and now it was bearing rich fruit. Louise and I praised God; this was fulfillment of our main purpose in traveling around the world. Our goal was not just to win a few souls, but to help plant the indigenous church and see it become a healthy national organism bringing Christ to the nations.

On the last leg of our honeymoon mission, we flew from Lima on a Douglas DC-4 to Guayaquil, Ecuador, for meetings, then across the gulf toward the Panama Canal Zone. We soon lost sight of the great South American continent with its seven million square miles. But we knew we had left behind a host of friends, and we took with us lifelong memories of blessings. The shape of the continent made us think of it as a heart pulsating with vigorous vitality, yearning to know the truth that sets men free.

By noon that day we were within sight of the Panama Canal. From our altitude we could see the fifty miles from the Atlantic to the Pacific as the giant, four-engine plane soared overhead three times waiting its turn to land at Balboa. Panama, resplendent in the brilliant sunshine, presented one of the most beautiful and memorable sights we had seen. We had time to lounge around in the city for a few hours.

Once again we boarded the plane headed for Guatemala in Central America, where we deplaned long enough for us to rush over to the church there and speak before returning and heading for New Orleans.

It was dark when the great plane nosed out across the Gulf of Mexico toward New Orleans. Below we could see fires built by the Indians who were burning their lands preparatory to planting on the hillsides. Sleep would not come; we were too excited. Our great honeymoon adventure was ending. In a way we were sad. However, we had worked hard, and the travel had been exhausting. According to my wife's carefully kept statistics, in the twenty countries and islands we had visited and the approximately one hundred towns in which we ministered, more than two thousand immortal souls had responded to our invitation to accept Christ as Savior. How many more than that had their eyes opened to the truth would remain known only to God. We had witnessed to white, black, brown, yellow, and red men from Halifax to Buenos Aires, with no respect of persons.

In our private devotions, Louise and I had read the Bible through, from Genesis through Revelation. Louise had sung in English in the Virgin Islands and Trinidad; she had sung in Portuguese in Brazil and Spanish in other countries. My messages had to be interpreted from place to place. It had indeed been fifty thousand miles of missionary miracles. The first chapter of our adventure as man and wife together was about to close. The second chapter was about to begin. It had been over a year since we had left the same airport in New Orleans for Miami and the West Indies. The war was over. Now we were home. The greatest adventures of our life were yet ahead of us.

20

A Time of Adjustment

Louise and I were expecting our first baby and needed a place to call home. We bought a little house in Springfield, Missouri, which became our headquarters for the next several months as we continued speaking throughout America at conventions, camp meetings, and missionary engagements. Our first child, Frank, was born in Springfield on December 31, 1946. I was almost thirty-five years old.

During this time of seeking God's guidance for our lives as a family, I had the opportunity to revisit Europe. Taking the R.M.S. *Queen Mary* I sailed for Southampton, England, where I was shocked to see the destruction, especially where bombs had made direct hits on the Hampstead Bible Institute in London, effectively destroying it. The reunion with Howard Carter was a special time. He had escaped injury, but the emotional stress on him and the people of England was obvious—many of them still seemed dazed.

I took the night boat from Dover to France, where I

revisited a number of the churches and pastors I had seen in better times. In Normandy I wept to see the beach where our fighting men had landed and so many had died. Here, as elsewhere, entire towns had been erased from the face of the earth. It was a time of adjustment worldwide; and in my own private world of thoughts I was doing much praying, studying the Bible, and seeking the will of the Lord.

From France I went by train across Switzerland into Italy. I was thankful for opportunities to speak to weary souls throughout many of these cities in Europe. But God was doing a work in my own heart, too. It was during this time that God began to urge upon me a plan for reaching the multitudes. I had been preaching since I was seventeen years of age, and I'd been a missionary since I was twenty. As I thought about the things I'd observed on my missionary travels, I realized that from 50 to 60 percent of all the nations in the world have one large city. If you were to raise up a great evangelistic center in that major city, you could touch the nation for Christ.

I had seen every kind of missionary work under the sun. I was often excited and disturbed at the same time. Many times I felt discouraged and weary and my heart was broken. There was so much work to do and so few willing to do it. I had been in Shanghai, for instance, in a little church that seated about fifty people; but outside were six million Chinese souls in one city. I can't tell you how that burdened me. I knew that was repeated in many places throughout the world—I'd been there.

I knew that many of the great cities of the world were virtually untouched with the gospel message. When I went through Central America, there wasn't a single

Full-Gospel church in any capital of the six republics. When I talked about this to our mission boards, asking them why they didn't go to the great cities, they would reply, "Brother Sumrall, it costs too much." I boiled on the inside like a volcano when I heard such weak excuses.

I returned to the United States with a renewed vision and dedication. The Lord had shown me three things about reaching the nations for Him: *First*, we were to bind the powers of the devil operating in the land. There is a compelling need on the mission field to shackle the powers of Satan and set people free. Jesus said to first bind the strong man (see Matt. 12:29). *Second*, after the people are set free from Satan's power, the new converts must be taught and settled in God's Word. The fruits of a revival must be preserved. And *third*, going into the capital cities, the heart, or the core, of a country and erecting evangelistic centers would enable the people to be grounded in the Word. Then they could go back to their towns and villages to win their kinsmen to Christ and establish their own indigenous churches.

Once back in the states, I was asked to conduct a revival in Memphis, Tennessee. While there a call came to pastor a church in South Bend, Indiana. I had conducted successful revival crusades there several times in the past at the South Bend Gospel Tabernacle. But to be truthful, when the call came I wasn't too impressed. I just didn't think there was any reason why the Lord would want me to settle down in such an unobtrusive town in the snow belt of America.

A second and a third call from the South Bend people finally got me down on my knees pleading with God to give me direction. The South Bend people told me they had fasted and prayed and that the Lord had impressed upon them the need to remind me of their needs. The Lord confirmed that the call really was His and that the South Bend church was to be my training ground to accomplish the goals the Lord had set on my heart.

In early December Louise and I and our baby son arrived at our first pastorate. We assembled in a miserable, run-down, low-ceilinged building big enough to hold at most 165 people. The casement windows squeaked, the roof leaked, and the wind whistled through the building. I surveyed the situation and advised the congregation that I felt we should sell the building and start over. We moved into a large tent and held evangelistic services for eleven weeks. By the end of summer we had three times more people than when we began. God had blessed this venture of faith.

We bought a lot on the corner of Michigan and Ewing, one of the finest intersections of the city of South Bend, and were able to raise the $35,000 to pay for the lot. We then began to build. It was amazing to see God leading us step by step and supplying our every need as we followed what we felt to be His direction.

When winter came, we rented the third floor in a downtown building. By spring the back part of our new church building was completed and we moved in. By summer we were able to occupy our new auditorium that seated a thousand. We named the new church Calvary Temple.

Rex Humbard and his family came to preach a revival for us, and we gained more new members. Oral Roberts, Clifton Erickson, William Branham, and many other evangelists came to help us. We rented city buses to bring

160

people to the Sunday services. God helped us to capture the imagination of the people of the city, and we had over a hundred Sunday school classes. The church expanded so fast that we never stopped building.

At the same time we were building the work in South Bend, I continued to be involved in missionary work around the world. In 1950, I took a six-week missionary tour once again to Europe, Africa, and the Orient; and I went to Israel, Egypt, and India for the first time. Charles Blair and Ernie Rebb accompanied me on this trip. We usually conducted three-day city-wide crusades.

The highlight of this trip was the crusade in Manila, the Philippines. This capital city was the home of several million souls. I was astonished that in this "Pearl of the Orient" there was not one aggressive Full-Gospel church, even though Full-Gospel missions surrounded it in the countryside.

Most of the downtown government building still showed the signs of battle. The awful marks of war had left the city scarred and with a broken spirit. We rented Rizal Stadium and saw hundreds respond as we gave the call to give their hearts to Christ. But when we left, I was once again burdened—we had to leave them without leadership or a place to meet for worship.

Back in South Bend, where the work was growing and prospering, we were able to buy ten acres of land and a lovely home on East Ireland, at the time a country road. Not long afterward, having comfortably settled in and having consolidated the church and paid off its indebtedness, we were conducting a successful missionary convention when the Lord spoke to my heart.

The world harvest was never out of my mind, and about

three o'clock that Sunday afternoon of the convention, I was reminded of my long ago tormenting vision of the world going to hell. The voice of the Lord wasn't audible, but I knew He was saying to me, "Lester, will you go to Manila for Me?"

I found myself arguing with that still, small, inner voice. "But Lord, the work is so great here in South Bend now. You called me to this city, and I haven't finished my work here."

God doesn't argue, but His gentle nudging is persistent. "Lester, will you go to Manila for Me?"

I felt honored and humbled by this pressure of divine destiny. Ecstasy flooded my soul like a river of heavenly blessing. The Spirit witnessed to my heart that I was to say yes to God, that this was the will of God for Louise and me. We now had two sons, for on June 27, 1950, God had given us our second boy, Stephen. I came downstairs, embraced Louise, and said, "Darling, we are going to Manila. God has assured me this is His will for us."

Her first word was, "When?"

Our church board and congregation found it difficult to believe at first, but they could see that the call of Manila burned hot within my bosom. Before us was the challenge of one of the world's great cities.

21

A Heart for Missions

Sailing from San Francisco on the Swedish freighter the S.S. *Wangaretta* in the summer of 1952, we were twenty-two days on the high seas before arriving in the Philippine archipelago.

Our contacts had rented an abandoned vegetable market in Tondo, one of the worst slums in the city of Manila, about eight miles from the center of the town. It was an open, iron-bar structure with walls made of banana leaves woven through loose wires. It stood next to an open drainage ditch. When I first saw it, two bloated, dead hogs were lying in the ditch, covered with flies. The stench was almost unbearable. The forty people present for the first service had to cover their noses with bandanas. Twenty-five of the forty were students from a local Bible school, and the others were visitors from nearby churches. No unsaved people were in that audience insofar as we could tell. I was so discouraged. This was quite an adjustment after leaving the work in South Bend.

The Philippines had never had a great revival. Three hundred years ago when the Spanish arrived, they brought the Roman Catholic religion to the completely pagan country. Then in 1898, when Admiral George Dewey drove out the Spanish, he made way for the Protestants. The Methodist missionaries did a marvelous job setting up schools and educating the people. Still, there had never been a true revival in the land.

But my heart was in the bustling, throbbing city of Manila. The city was where the teeming masses of people were. We began to pray and ask the Lord for property in the middle of town on which to build an evangelistic center. It was obvious we would never establish a strong, indigenous church without a more desirable location. I began to look for a downtown lot on which to build such a center, even before I had a congregation. I was certain God had sent me to build an evangelistic center in the heart of Manila. And then I found it—two blocks from the legislative buildings, near the YMCA, the Red Cross building, and the offices of the American Bible Society. It was at Taft Avenue and United Nations Street, one of the busiest thoroughfares in the city, and it had already been cleared for us by a World War II bomb!

With the help of the Rev. Paul Pipkin and friends back home, the $20,000 necessary to purchase this choice piece of property was secured.

We found the Filipinos a very difficult people. We didn't know what time to have church, as the people's concept of time was far different from ours. Those first six months in Manila were extremely frustrating. I tried to absorb the Filipino's thinking so as to be better able to communicate with them. Jesus came from heaven to identify with us and our problems; I could do no less for those to whom He had sent me.

Now that we had the lot, we needed a building. I finally discovered an old, unused, steel, B-52 airplane hangar worth about $50,000 being stored in a large garage owned by the Pepsi Cola Company. We were able to purchase it for $10,000. When we brought it to the downtown property, it covered almost every square inch from property line to property line. We then hired a fine architect to design the front and the interior, a forty-foot cathedral dome, and forty-foot steel and glass windows on each side with a large sign over the entrance that read: Bethel Temple—Christ Is the Answer.

We then made arrangements to hold a city-wide crusade at the San Lazaro race track. American evangelist A. C. Valdez, Jr., had sent word that he would come and hold this for us. We posted signs, handed out handbills, and took an ad in the Manila *Times* that went to all the islands of the country.

The opening service saw about twelve hundred people present. Each night the crowd grew larger until we were drawing about five thousand every night. Many people came forward nightly for salvation; and after every service we prayed for the sick and suffering until well past midnight. We announced a water baptism for the final Sunday afternoon. Thousands showed up. That afternoon, 359 men and women were baptized, and out of that group our church in Manila was born.

But before we completed and moved into our new facility, I would have one of the most astonishing experiences of my life. It was a miracle that was the key to a spiritual revival that would shake the Philippines. Manila would never be the same again.

One evening following the news the announcer said, "Good evening, ladies and gentlemen. If you have a weak heart, please turn your radio off!"

I had a strong heart. Reaching for the radio dial, I turned the volume up. Suddenly a series of piercing screams blared through the radio speaker, followed by pandemonium. "Help me, help me. They are killing me!" It was the cry of a woman.

In the background, voices of several men could be heard through the confusion—"This can all be explained. . . . This is epilepsy. . . . This is extreme hysteria."

I could hear others saying, "She is blue in the face. . . . There are marks on her neck."

Someone else cried out, "Look, the marks of teeth appear!" Then I heard the girl scream again. Such a haunting, tormenting scream it was—the scream of a girl possessed. I had heard those screams before; I had dealt with those who were demon-possessed before.

The announcer explained that they were in Bilibid Prison and that Clarita Villanueva, a young, provincial girl, had been picked up in the streets of Manila for vagrancy and she claimed she was being attacked by demons. She had displayed several bite marks all over her body. Twenty-five witnesses, including Manila's chief of police, Col. Cesar Lucero, said that it was a very realistic example of a horrified woman being bitten to insanity by "invisible persons."

I jumped out of bed and found myself standing in the middle of the room. Evidently a feisty little newsman had stuck his microphone right in the middle of the melee.

Turning to my wife I said, "That woman is demon-possessed. That's the kind of thing I found in Java, China, and Europe. Yes, and I found it in America, too. It's horrible, Louise. Honey, try to get some sleep. I'm going into the front room."

I lay down on the floor and began to weep before the Lord for that little human being who was being destroyed in such a savage manner. I couldn't get away from the sound of her blood-curdling screams. I continued praying, asking God to cast out the devils and deliver her. Early in the morning God impressed upon my heart that I was to go to the city jail, and He would use me to deliver her.

At first I strongly resisted the idea of going to the prison and seeking out the authorities and asking them to take me to this young woman. The announcer had said that doctors, scientists, professors, legal experts, and even spiritualists had tried to help her, but to no avail. But I have learned that where God's finger points, there His hand will make a way.

My architect friend accompanied me to the mayor's office. The mayor then contacted Dr. Mariano Lara, chief medical adviser of the Manila Police Department. Not long thereafter I found myself seated alongside Dr. Lara, who said that in his thirty-eight years of medical practice he had performed over eight thousand autopsies and had never found a devil yet. But he couldn't understand this baffling Filipino girl's being bitten by unseen assailants, and it was changing his philosophy of life. "I am humble enough to admit that I am a frightened man," he said.

My first hurdle was to convince this Dr. Lara that I

knew what I was doing and could help the girl. Opening my Bible, I read to him from the gospel of Mark, chapter 16, verse 17: "And these signs shall follow them that believe; In my name shall they cast out devils." Dr. Lara was open-minded enough to understand the truth of the Word of God, and permission was granted for me to see Clarita.

When Clarita first saw me, her eyes widened and she snarled at me and hissed, "I don't like you." I recognized that it was Satan speaking through her lips. A holy anointing came upon me, and I entered into the greatest spiritual battle of my life. I was angry at Satan, and I rebuked him in the name of Jesus.

We were surrounded by friendly onlookers who I sensed possessed hope, if not faith, that God's power in me would deliver this pathetic young girl from demonic control. Satan blasphemed through Clarita's lips and cursed the blood of Jesus in the vilest language.

I was soaked with perspiration and exhausted. With hot tears streaking her flushed face, Clarita begged us to leave her alone. I saw the teeth marks on her neck and arms and knew this was not going to be an easy battle. Again Clarita became Satan's mouthpiece as the demons cried through her, "Go away! Go away!"

I decided I needed to get alone with the Lord, I needed time to fast and pray; so I requested that I be allowed to return the following day. The observers had tears in their eyes in the face of such suffering. I thanked them for their kindness, concern, and prayers. I asked them to continue to intercede on my behalf and assured them I would be back.

The Manila papers carried the story that night. And the

extra day of fasting and prayer made the difference. As I commanded the demons to come out, they seemed to realize it was their last struggle. They cursed and screamed; but suddenly Clarita relaxed, and I felt she was released. The glazed look left her eyes, she smiled, and an indescribable peace enveloped all of us. I asked Clarita if the demons were gone and she answered weakly, "Yes."

"Where did they go?"

She turned her head and pointed toward the steel-barred window.

Through an interpreter I explained to Clarita what had happened. I told her she needed to pray and ask God for forgiveness of her sins, invite Jesus Christ into her life, and receive Him as Savior and Lord. I was able to spend some time with her, instructing her from the Bible and showing her that the blood of Jesus had cleansed her. I told her that the demons might make one more attempt to victimize her and that if this happened, she must demand them to leave "in Jesus' name."

Clarita was delivered miraculously, and Dr. Lara triumphantly declared, "The devils are gone."

God used this to open up the city of Manila to receiving His Word. Our ministry and work became known all over the Philippines. People began to understand that there is more to religion than church services, more to Christianity than pomp, parades, and gaudy garments. It was unsought publicity, but God surely used it for good and to accomplish His perfect will.

Permits for completion of our church building had been held up in the mayor's office. Now, within ten minutes, we had the blueprints and permits signed and handed over to us.

"What else can we do for you?" the mayor asked.

"I need a place to tell the people what God has done for Clarita. I would like to use the Sunken Gardens across the street in Roxas Park for a crusade." The park was strategically situated and was known to everyone in the Philippines. Arrangements were made for us to use the park for one month, and we converted it into a great outdoor cathedral.

God sent a team of Christians to assist us—students from Bethel Bible Institute, Christians from the Methodist church, professional people in the media, class-A airtime paid for by the Rev. David Candelaria and the Methodist church of Taytay, and the Rev. Clifton Erickson as evangelist to help minister to the masses of people who were expected.

News spread like wildfire that meetings were going to take place in the Sunken Gardens, where a huge sign proclaimed CHRIST IS THE ANSWER.

By noon each day the people began to congregate in Roxas Park. When the service got into full swing each evening, the park was a sea of faces, sometimes thirty thousand and more. They came from every city and province, from the villages and neighboring islands. They came by boat, in trucks, in carts, on mules—walking, riding—every way a human being can travel. They came and they returned to their homes with the message that Christ is the answer.

Oral Roberts's ministry had sent its film *Venture into Faith*, which was shown in Manila and many places throughout the islands.

Gordon Lindsay of Dallas, Texas, felt led by God to send thousands of issues of his magazine, *The Voice of*

Healing. The mass distribution of deliverance literature was, we felt, a contributing factor to the revival. Although the more sensational ministry of deliverance no doubt helped draw the crowds to the meetings, the salvation of souls was our top priority. My consuming passion was to see souls rescued from hell. And God honored and blessed; the response was simply overwhelming.

One night a thunderstorm interrupted the service, but hardly a person moved. The people had come prepared, and the sea of faces became a sea of brightly colored umbrellas. Thousands made decisions for Christ.

One night I spoke plainly to the men, explaining what it meant to become a real Christian. I talked about living holy lives—stopping drinking, going to movies, gambling at the cock fights, cheating on their wives—and that they would be expected to change their life-style and cultivate the habits of prayer, Bible reading, and church attendance. When I asked those to come forward who wanted to live this kind of life, I was unprepared for the response—they came, five thousand strong they came! It was one of the greatest moments of my ministry. How I praised and thanked God!

As a result of that revival, Bethel Temple became the largest Protestant church in the Orient. The enthusiasm of these people is hard to capture in words on paper. When we received the new church members, it took a whole month for us to instruct them on what it means to be a Christian and how to walk the Christian walk. Baptism followed.

Soon we had ten thousand people registered in our Sunday school. To accommodate the crowds, we had Sunday school on Saturday afternoon as well as four services on Sunday. Church would begin at 7:00 A.M. and continue until late Sunday evening. The B-52 hangar was packed to overflowing at every service.

We had to add full-time pastors to the staff to minister to those who spoke various dialects. Services were held in Ilocano and in Tagalog, each with its own pastor, and I preached to the English-speaking congregation and also to the Chinese with the aid of an interpreter.

We completed Bethel Temple through a series of financial miracles. The results of that great revival extended beyond the capital city of Manila. Soon Bethel Temple became a "mother" church for a second church in Quezon City, a third in Niac, a fourth in Pasig, and a fifth in Caloocan. Branch Sunday schools, outstations, and other preaching centers followed.

We invited Oral Roberts to come to Manila for another crusade in Roxas Park, and we took him to meet President Magsaysay, who looked at him and said, "In this country we have learned that Christ *is* the answer."

The end of this great move of God was nowhere in sight. I fully expected to remain in Manila for a very long time. But God had other plans.

During all the excitement and activity, the Lord blessed us with Peter, our third son, on October 17, 1953.

Then God began to deal with my heart about leaving the Philippines in the height of revival there. "Why, Lord?" I protested. "Look at what is going on here."

"That's the reason," I sensed the Lord saying. "The Oriental people are beginning to worship you instead of Me."

What had been happening was this: The people were extremely devoted to my spiritual leadership, so much so that many times they would fall on their knees and kiss my hands before I could stop them. People would recognize me on the street, at the post office, or in some public place and fall out of line to allow me to move ahead of them. I didn't like it; it made me uncomfortable, and I knew what the Bible plainly taught: God is to receive the honor and glory. But how could I convey this to these people? I sensed that the best thing to do would be for us to think of leaving. I was to be a pioneer, not a resident pastor. "Lord," I prayed, "there must be a further reason for You to want us to leave. Tell me what we are to do next."

Yes, there was another reason. Within the next two weeks I received a cable from America. We were needed back at the South Bend church.

22

Feed Your Faith
and Starve Your Doubts

We had moved to Manila with equipment and supplies to begin the work there in good shape. When we returned to the United States, we carried only our personal belongings in our suitcases. Freely we had received at the hand of the Lord and God's faithful people, freely we would give. Thousands were at the Manila airport to see us off. We left amid many tears and the warm embraces of these people whom we had come to love so very much. They in turn loved us. But we left confident that we were doing God's will and knowing that the work was in the hands of fine pastors. Publicly and privately we had taught the people that their greatest love was to be for the Lord Jesus and that their security was in Him and not in any human being.

Returning to South Bend seemed almost like a dream. It was like we had never been away. The church needed us. The pastor who had followed me had moved on elsewhere, and it seemed right and good to be back among these faithful people. The crowds surged, the work expanded, and the blessings of God were evident upon the church and her people. At the same time, the congregation understood my calling and burden for world evangelism and gave me freedom in traveling and ministering in various parts of the world.

On a Saturday morning in 1956, I sensed that the Lord was once again speaking to me about another city where there was work to be done for Him. This time it was Jerusalem. So it was that in August of that year I took a six-month leave of absence from the South Bend pastorate and moved my family almost six thousand miles to the Holy City. While there I served as pastor in one of the churches and held "Prophecy Rallys" in the Jerusalem YMCA building.

It wasn't easy, we discovered, to witness to the Jew; but my wife, as in other places, proved to be a real asset for the work and a blessing and help to many. I think it was in Jerusalem that we both really began to understand about feeding our faith and starving our doubts. God gave us ample opportunity to exercise our faith. We found that many of the Jewish people didn't even believe in the God of the Old Testament, so how could they believe in the Son of God! Ours was a real teaching ministry, often on a one-to-one basis.

Early one morning I walked the few blocks from where we were living to a craggy rock overhanging the Valley of Hinnom. From there I could see Zion's hill, the ancient walls of Old Jerusalem, the Wailing Wall, the Mount of Olives with the Garden of Gethsemane, and the road to Bethlehem. I had gone there to pray, and there God spoke to my heart. "Lester, you are responsible for taking one million souls to heaven."

It was a precious time as I alternately prayed and sought to hear God's still small voice deep in the inner recesses of my heart. I asked Him, "God, how is that possible?" Humanly, I staggered at the task.

Quietly, as I sat there alone communing with the Lord, into my mind He put these thoughts: It was the idea of two plowmen, one plowing deep, the other wide. Deep was my responsibility; wide the opportunity. I was to share the vision with partners of the same spirit and spread the gospel message by utilizing the mass media, the written word, full-time gospel radio, deliverance films, and whatever means would come my way in the ensuing years. I was reminded of the millions of depressed and possessed human beings who needed deliverance from satanic forces. And once again my mind returned to my long-ago vision of souls on the road to hell. This was my calling, and I would be true to it.

One weekend we were sightseeing in Tiberias near the Sea of Galilee. We had rented a little house and were sleeping on the bottom floor just below ground level. All night long we heard rumbling like thunder, yet it was different. I turned to my wife and said, "Honey, that's not normal. Something unusual is happening." We remembered that earlier in the afternoon we had noticed many of the young men rushing from their homes and shops as if they were in a terrible hurry to get somewhere. We didn't get much sleep the rest of that night and early morning. When we got up we realized that the rumbling noise had been heavy trucks speeding down the road; and when we returned to Jerusalem, we saw what seemed to be thousands of tanks, covered with camouflage, on their way to meet the Egyptian invaders. Israel had entered what became known as the Sinai War. We lived through this nightmarish time of blackouts and terror.

On Monday we sent our sons to the British school they attended. Usually there were three hundred students, but that day our boys returned saying they were the only ones who had gone to school. Everyone, it seemed, had evacuated—even the American ambassador was gone. Insofar as we knew, we were the only family of Americans left in that part of Jerusalem. But God had sent me to Israel for six months, and I wasn't going to leave just because they were having a war. Anyway, it made no difference to me if my family and I went to heaven from Israel or from the United States!

I applied for and received permission from the government to travel through the battle zone as a press correspondent. During this time I wrote numerous magazine and newspaper articles about the Israeli-Egyptian conflict in the light of Bible prophecy. And I began publishing my own prophecy newsletter, which was circulated around the world.

In March 1957, when the second Arab-Israeli war was over, so was our leave. We returned to our church in South Bend; but after having heard from God in what I felt was such a definite leading while seated on the rock overlooking the city, my mind was in a whirl. There was so much to do—increase the publication and circulation of literature, produce deliverance films, and increase our radio ministry. There was also the congregation in South Bend that needed the leading of a pastor who was there.

23

The Island Metropolis in Need of a Church

God continued to bless our work in South Bend, but I could not reconcile myself to the fact that my ministry for God was to be confined to a local congregation. The church had given its blessings to my travel in the past, and now once again I left for Hong Kong with Gordon Lindsay (Christ for the Nations) and Morris Cerullo to conduct crusades on this great island metropolis.

You will remember that Howard Carter and I had spent a brief time in Hong Kong many years earlier on our trips into mainland China. Now the doors into China were closed. And I had the strong feeling that if only a church could be established in Hong Kong, this church could be a lighthouse when the doors into China once again swung open. I went to my knees about this: "Lord, do You want us to start such a church as we did in Manila? Do you want us to help train the Chinese here in Hong Kong so they will be ready to go into the mainland of China when the time is ripe?"

Just about this time A. C. Valdez, the evangelist who held the first city-wide crusade for us in Manila, came to me and encouraged me to begin such a work in Hong Kong, the hub of the Orient. After much fasting and prayer and talking this over with Louise, we both felt that God was directing us in this new venture of faith.

In 1959 I resigned my pastorate in South Bend for the second time and moved my family to Hong Kong, into an apartment on the side of Victoria Peak. Frank was twelve years old; Steven, nine; and Peter, six. I was forty-six.

In downtown Hong Kong we bought the fourth floor of a new office building located on the waterfront adjacent to the post office. Amazingly, in the same building the Communist party occupied the seventh floor, the Roman Catholics had the third floor, and many other organizations and businesses shared the remainder of the building. We converted our floor into an auditorium that would seat about three hundred people and named it "New Life Temple." We were helped by a half-dozen men from the Hong Kong chapter of the Full-Gospel Businessmen's Fellowship International and began with sixty-nine charter members, including some who had come forward at one of our crusades (prior to making our move) and had given their hearts to the Lord.

Our congregation was made up primarily of people who had fled out of the southern part of China when the Communists took over. Over half the people in Hong Kong were refugees. People were constantly trying to reach Hong Kong from the Chinese mainland, some of them making it by swimming from the Kwangtung coast of southern China. We had a congregation of people who knew what sorrowing and suffering were. They knew what it meant to be persecuted, abused, and deprived. They clung to their freedom dearly.

We ministered three times weekly to three totally dissimilar Chinese congregations. On Sunday mornings the wealthiest, upper-class people came. They needed Jesus, too. On Sunday evenings some of the poorest people I've ever seen came; these included the refugees. On Friday evenings the small businessmen and their families worshiped with the boat people—those whose entire lives were spent afloat in a junk or sampan. But, most importantly, God was in our midst, helping us to do that which was unusual for Hong Kong. Many miracles occurred—remarkable healings—and conversions. Our main goal was to win men and women to Christ and to draw families to the Lord.

New Life Temple didn't become as large as Bethel Temple in Manila, but it became a very strong evangelistic center that remains to this day. And it also became the mother church to a second congregation.

In Hong Kong we annually printed and distributed over one million books, tracts, and pamphlets in the Chinese language that were distributed in Singapore, Indonesia, the Philippines, Taiwan, and Malaysia. Not only that, but we also shuttled the hour-and-a-half flight to Manila, where I was able to help with the work there. And during that time we were able to start three more churches in the Philippines. We also found time in our rigorous schedule to conduct several revival meetings throughout the Orient—Malaysia, Java, Singapore, and Bangkok, Thailand.

Seeing the impact of the printed word gave impetus to

starting *World Harvest* magazine, our official journal centered on the person of Jesus Christ, exalting Him and His mighty deliverance offered to all who will believe and accept Him.

I began to sense that it was time for us to establish a home base of operations. Our outreach now embraced crusade evangelism, literature outreach, and a growing interest in a radio ministry. Thus it was that in April 1962, we moved back to South Bend to the property we had bought some years earlier. We bought an IBM typewriter, a printing press, and some second-hand mailing equipment. Then we hired a printer, a secretary, an editor, and a mail clerk and set about to publish the second issue of *World Harvest* magazine.

I had seen the results that could be achieved through the printing of literature. In 1944 my first book, *Through Blood and Fire*, had been published by Zondervan Publishing House. This was followed in 1948 by *50,000 Miles of Missionary Miracles* (also published by Zondervan). Following that, several smaller books had been published. While in Hong Kong I wrote and had published the booklet *Destroying Your Deadliest Enemy*. I recognized that books, booklets, pamphlets, tracts, and magazines could often go where pastors, evangelists, missionaries, and writers of Christian literature cannot physically go. Surely this is one of the ways God would have us reach millions yet unreached for Him. I said to my wife, "Louise, we can have a world pulpit through the printed page."

24

The Cry of a Native Son

America was in worse condition than the Philippines in the mid-1960s, a time that will go down as one of the darkest hours in our national history. Unrestrained madness was erupting with a fury on university campuses across the land. Violence was rampant at political rallies and conventions—as in Chicago. God had revealed a scenario to me in my mind's eye that I was not witnessing firsthand on the streets of our country. The rioting, the burning of buildings, the drug culture, the sexual revolution, the "hippies," the homosexuality—all of these things and more I saw through tear-filled eyes. It was a new generation of Americans whose life-style was consumed with sin, sickness, and a preoccupation with a form of degrading madness.

I wrote these words that summed up my feelings upon our return. They appeared on the front cover of the September 1965 issue of our *World Harvest* magazine:

The Cry of a Native Son

America, I love you.

I am a son of your native soil.

I am most at home in your big cities.

I have drunk deeply of your freedoms.

I have enjoyed your abundance.

But, America, can you not see the "handwriting
on the wall"?

Your enemies are deadly within and without.

You have poisonous vipers posing as your friends.

They are ready for a fatal thrust.

America, you bear the hatred of many lands.

I have heard you cursed in foreign tongues.

I have seen you misunderstood by men and nations.

You are unloved and unwanted in a world of
peril and need.

America, worst of all, you are sick inside.

I see your newsstands filled with pornographic
reading.

I see your clothes styled by sex deviates.

I see your lust for pleasure like a Roman delight.

America, I see you worshiping the golden calf of
material greed.

You need Christ . . . NOW.

You need His love, His delivering power.

America, it may not be too late for you to find
God now.

God save America—land that I love.

God had told me that America needed my help. "Lord,
how can I help my country?" He had promised He would
show me. Now, back in this country, I waited on Him to
make known His will for the future of my work and my
family and myself.

In South Bend a minister friend shook his head at me and pronounced, "Lester Sumrall, you're fifty and you're finished!"

"If you were God," I answered him, "I would believe you, but you're not God."

But that sent me to my knees in prayer. "Lord, I know I'm fifty, but I can't believe You've sent me back here to do nothing. Show me what You want us to do."

Deep within, in that beautiful, quiet way the Lord has of letting His children know they are loved and what His will is for us, I heard, "Lester, you have just begun. Your life and ministry are before you."

In the Philippines God had spoken to my heart about the sleeping giant of television and how it could be used to reach the world for Him. At the time I had said, "God, I'll put a television program for You on the air," but the inaudible voice of God directed, "No, I'm not talking about that. You'll have to own the stations. A network of TV stations is needed as a channel of truth to America. You will do it."

Now, as my mind replayed that previous quiet-time with the Lord, and as I sensed His encouragement, I knew that I must accept the challenge of pioneering Christian television and getting on with the work of LeSea (the name of our ministry) as an ongoing arm of worldwide outreach for the Lord. But it would once again begin in South Bend.

One day a petition was handed to me with sixty-nine signatures and the request that we start a church of divine deliverance and power in the South Bend area. God gave peace to our hearts as we contemplated whether this was what we should do. One of the ways we can know we are following God's leading and doing His will is when we experience that settled peace as we pray and seek His will. My thoughts were directed to Jeremiah 33:9, where I read:

> And it shall be to me a name of joy, a praise and an honour before all the nations of the earth, which shall hear all the good that I do unto them: and they shall fear and tremble for all the goodness and for all the prosperity that I procure unto it.

I felt confident that South Bend was to be the base for LeSea from which we could have a worldwide outreach. I began to preach everywhere there was an invitation. I appealed for help to our friends throughout the world— *World Harvest* magazine was being sent to people in 107 nations.

In 1966, with meager funds in the bank, I signed my name to a contract to begin construction of a building on East Ireland Road to house LeSea headquarters and the church. This was the property we had acquired a few years before. Now we made the decision, as a family, to donate the house and land to the church. Plans were completed to build a thousand-seat auditorium. We didn't have much in the way of financial resources, but we had God's promise that we had only just begun our world ministry. He owns the cattle on a thousand hills (see Ps. 50:10), all things were made by Him (see John 1:3), we are His children and heirs of God and joint-heirs with Christ (see Rom. 8:17); therefore, we had nothing to fear.

One morning my telephone rang. I was surprised to hear the voice of Elva Soriano, calling from the Philippines. Her orphanage for headhunter children (which had begun with twelve whom she personally had adopted) had grown beyond her ability to support all its needs. God had already been dealing with me about the world's starving children; so I said, "Elva, a check will be on its way this morning as soon as I get to the office."

That was the beginning of another arm of our work, the World Harvest Homes. From that small beginning this work extended into various tribes in the Philippines, then to Hong Kong, and later into Israel, Italy, and India. Today we are supporting over 1000 children in thirteen nations with a total of fifteen homes. This is a part of our ministry that is ever expanding, because the needs worldwide are so great.

One day the church building was an empty shell. The walls and roof were up, but that was as far as our money would go. As I stood inside those four walls that cold, rainy day, wondering how God would supply, the vice-president of the American National Bank in South Bend came wading through the mud. "I'm looking for Lester Sumrall," he said. I told him I was the man. We shook hands and he proceeded to say, "Do you have a loan on this building?"

"No, sir," I replied. I didn't tell him how desperate our situation was or that we had no collateral. I had raised my family in the Philippines on about a hundred dollars a month, and my wife and I had learned how to stretch a dollar. But I didn't fill him in on all those details.

"I represent the American National Bank. We'd like to loan you the money. In return, we'd like you to move your business to our bank. How much do you need to complete this building?"

"One hundred forty thousand." I knew exactly what was needed.

"We're prepared to finance that amount. Come on down to the bank and let's get started."

From that moment on we experienced the kind of miraculous financing that was always needed in order to move the Lord's work along. The building was completed and officially dedicated on Easter Sunday 1967.

Even before organizing what became known as the Christian Center Church in South Bend, we began petitioning the Federal Communications Commission for a construction permit for a new FM radio station. It was while we were building our new church that the permit came from the FCC. Now we needed the money to put up a tower and studio facilities for what we had decided would be called WHME (World Harvest Missionary Evangelism). I consulted with my business manager—that's the Lord—and asked, "Lord, how are we going to get the money to build this station?" And in my heart I heard, "Sign for it."

We bought land on Highway 23 and began accepting bids for the tower, antenna, and transmitter. A nice brick building was constructed. Meanwhile, I pondered which bid to accept and once again experienced God's peace, which was the signal I needed. Before we knew it, there was our building, the tower, the antenna, and the transmitter—and we were on the air. Since that time WHME FM-103 has been reaching out to a fifty mile radius twenty-four hours a day, blessing multitudes of people with totally Christian programming.

While all this was going on, we were also producing documentary and dramatic gospel films featuring divine deliverance. We now have five such films in three languages, circulating in over fifty nations of the world. Non-promotional in nature, these films demonstrate the power

187

of God to set humanity free. Around the world these films are continuing to bring in a tremendous harvest of souls. We also began sending out cassette tapes of our messages, and the impact of this arm of our ministry has been phenomenal.

As I had been in prayer one day a few years before, the Lord had directed me to Psalm 71:18. I had asked God to reveal to me my future work. As I prayed, the power of the Lord came upon me. I felt an unusual anointing of the Holy Spirit. I opened my Bible and read: "Now also when I am old and greyheaded, O God, forsake me not; until I have shewed thy strength unto this generation, and thy power to every one that is to come."

Now the Lord brought that passage back to my mind as I began to realize that we needed help—pastors, missionaries, and evangelists who could minister worldwide in the power of God to help win the million the Lord had put on my heart. We needed a Bible school where we could train men and women. I saw Psalm 71:18 in the right perspective. Through our ministry we could train others and bring in students from across the nation as well as from Africa, Europe, India, Latin America, Israel, Hong Kong, Okinawa, the Philippines—from throughout the world.

The bank advanced the money, and we appealed to our friends worldwide once again. By faith we built our fine, functional, quarter-of-a-million-dollar facility that has a lecture hall, dining hall, dormitory rooms, and recreational area. Here we have our Advanced School of Evangelism and the World Harvest Bible College—a two-year training center providing preparation in the Word, plan, and work of God.

A few weeks after that I was in Washington, D.C., at a broadcaster's convention. A man walked up to me and said, "Dr. Sumrall, how would you like to have a television station?"

My mind said no because we were already as financially encumbered as I felt a ministry could be. But I heard the man out and learned that a bankrupt, million-watt television station licensed for the Indianapolis, Indiana, area was for sale. I assured the gentleman that I would pray about this and talk to our banker. Back in South Bend I approached the bank and made other necessary calls. After ten days of watching God move, working out all the details, we found ourselves with Channel 40-TV as our very own.

We began broadcasting on November 3, 1972, over WHMB (World Harvest Missionary Broadcasting) and began to see the blessing of God upon our efforts. Before long our ratings soared, souls were saved, and denominations began to flow together in friendliness and harmony. Today we are one of the best-equipped television facilities in the state of Indiana, with several million dollars worth of the best electronic gear available. Our daily "Today with Lester Sumrall" ninety-minute talk and call-in show averages four thousand letters and phone calls monthly. Still later we purchased Channel 46 in South Bend, a two-and-a-half-million-watt station, and renamed this station WHME (World Harvest Missionary Evangelism), the same as our radio station.

When we responded to the desperate need to provide Christian television programming, God's people responded. Each time when we signed the papers for loans, we had no idea where the money would come from. But I did know that God had called me to be a man of faith and to do a worldwide work for Him.

We did not know, for instance, that one bulb for our television operations costs as much as eighty dollars, and one light fixture as much as six hundred dollars. These were financial facts unknown to us that might have scared us off, humanly speaking.

God had shown me that Christian television could help to change a nation, and that our programs should also be sent to other large cities in the world. Thus it is that our programs can be seen in Tokyo and Manila, and every day in every way the men in our ministry are seeking new possibilities for reaching more people with the Good News of Jesus Christ.

Christian television is possibly one of the most powerful tools the Kingdom of God has ever had for getting people's attention, for turning them around and helping them to think and act according to biblical principles. At the time we went on the air there were only five or six such stations in the world. Today there are still only a dozen, and we still operate two of them. When I returned from Manila to labor for God in America, God promised me that on American television I would pray one short prayer and ten thousand souls could be set free from oppressive satanic bondage.

Jesus, in speaking to His disciples before ascending to be with the Father in heaven, said:

Go ye therefore, and teach all nations, baptizing them in the name of the Father, and of the Son, and of the Holy Ghost: Teaching them to observe all things whatsoever I have commanded you: and, lo, I am with you alway, even unto the end of the world (Matt. 28:19–20).

Surely, He must have had television in mind, for no other medium can penetrate so far, so well.

As our ministry grows, so do our sons. Peter, our youngest, is general manager of the radio and television stations. Frank is assistant pastor of Christian Center Church, and Stephen is president of LeSea, Inc. Our partners in this worldwide ministry are from every corner of the world.

Louise, like hundreds of dutiful and loving Christian wives and mothers, was always my strong support in my many ventures of faith. The Bible speaks of those who go down to battle and those who stay "by the stuff" (1 Sam. 30:24). It states plainly that "they shall share alike" (Amp. version). What a good wife she has been—raising our sons, staying behind to care for them while I took off to some needy place on the globe, and always maintaining a prayer vigil while I was out doing battle with the enemy!

All that has happened in our ministry and continues to happen is because everyone involved in it flows together in love. I can talk, I can preach, I can teach in person, and I can teach on video and cassette tape. One can plant the seed. Others must water by praying, giving, and working. Then it is God who gives the increase. Only together, in this way, can we realize a million or more souls landed safely in the arms of Jesus.